Advance Praise for
Hitchhiker in the Corner Office:

"Required reading for leaders, hiring managers, recruiters—and anyone interested in developing and retaining great talent."

—**David Peck, President of Leadership Unleashed®; Management Consulting and Coaching for Leaders**

*   *   *   *

"The Hitchhiker in the Corner Office tackles what is perhaps the greatest challenge facing our industry: the ability to retain talented people. It's a practical read full of real-world insights on how to ensure your business is more than just a quick pit stop on a great employee's journey to success."

—**Rick Van Warner, President of** *The Parquet Group*

*   *   *   *

"No other book provides such broad strategic overview and invaluable practical tips for today's employment landscape. Hitchhiker In The Corner Office is a must read for any executive entrenched in today's battle for the best talent."

—**David Gold, co-founder, Raleigh Group International and author of** *After the Absolute*

*   *   *   *

"Orrick ... is one of those rare recruiters that excels at recruiting and actually bothers to peek up over the office cubicle to see what others in the industry are or are not doing. I'm confident you will benefit greatly even if you

only apply a few of the excellent tips, techniques, and recommendations outlined in the pages that follow."

—Frank G. Risalvato, CPC, Founder of **www.searchwizardry.com**

* * * *

"Real world advice that professionals can apply immediately. Orrick's book is a must-read."

—**Marty Clarke, author of** Leadership Landmines **and** Communication Landmines

* * * *

"Hitchhiker capture's the mindset of today's job candidates and provides a fountain of great ideas on how to land them … and keep them!"

—**Joe Pelayo, C.P.C. author of** Work Your Network!

HITCHHIKER IN
THE CORNER OFFICE

HITCHHIKER IN THE CORNER OFFICE

Avoiding the Top-10 Hiring Potholes So
Your Employees Don't Hit the Road

Orrick G. Nepomuceno, CPC
Foreword by Frank G. Risalvato

iUniverse, Inc.
New York Lincoln Shanghai

Hitchhiker in the Corner Office
Avoiding the Top-10 Hiring Potholes So Your Employees Don't Hit the
Road

iUniverse books may be ordered through booksellers or by contacting:

iUniverse
2021 Pine Lake Road, Suite 100
Lincoln, NE 68512
www.iuniverse.com
1-800-Authors (1-800-288-4677)

ISBN-13: 978-0-595-43353-7 (pbk)
ISBN-13: 978-0-595-87679-2 (ebk)
ISBN-10: 0-595-43353-7 (pbk)
ISBN-10: 0-595-87679-X (ebk)

Printed in the United States of America

This book is dedicated to Kristen, Jack and Alina. You are my inspiration.

CONTENTS

▼

Acknowledgments

Writing this book was something that I have wanted to do for a very long time. But this book would not have been possible without the help of a lot of different people in my life; people to whom I sincerely owe a great amount of gratitude.

It is these folks that have been with me during my greatest moments and my lowest times, but became my friends and mentors regardless of where they met me along the journey.

Dick Wray: You gave me a chance and believed in me when no one else did. Thank you for offering a shoulder to lean on and an ear to listen to each day.

Bob Gershberg: Not only are you one of the greatest guys that I have met, but you are a mentor in every sense of the word. I know I can always depend on you for help.

David Ulrich: The true "Bull Dog"! You gave me a kick in the pants when I needed it the most. You Rock!

Lorana Price and Holy Cow! Team: Thank you for your help in developing a plan and direction for getting the message of this book out. You have been great to work with!

Rusty Fischer: Your sage wisdom and guidance made this book possible. I would not have been able to do it without you.

My children, Jack and Alina: You are the reason I wake up every day with a smile on my face. This book is for you.

And, last but not least, my wife, Kristen: You have stood by me and believed in my dreams. You are my best friend and I still cannot believe that you are still with me after all these years.

—Orrick Nepomuceno, CPC

A Brief Excerpt from
The Hitchhiker in the Corner Office

Hiring a merely mediocre employee can be costly. Hiring the first available employee instead of the best available can be even more so. How costly? The Wall Street Journal reports the total cost of executive employee turnover ranges from a low of 50% to 60% (The Hay Group) to 100% to 150% (Hewitt Associates) of the employee's yearly salary. These expenditures include training costs associated with new hires and the price of recruiting efforts required to replace employees.

Either way, the costs can be considerable. Factor in the time spent training a new employee and bring he or she up to speed, and you can quickly extrapolate out the collateral costs involved in merely losing one employee, let alone several.

To stop picking up hitchhikers and start hiring some talent who's willing to buckle up and stay the course, employers need to get real about their expectations with employees from day one.

What do you expect? What do they expect? These are not merely touchy-feely questions designed as time-filler during the interview; these are critical issues you both need to explore before ever sitting down in the first place. It is not enough to simply hire someone, expect them to leave after their four-year expiration date is up, and then give them a counteroffer to keep them from hitting the road.

A counteroffer will only keep an employee around until the next upwardly-mobile opportunity presents itself. Think of counteroffers as the rest stops along the hiring highway; your hitchhiker might stay in the corner office a little longer, but sooner or later a faster car or bigger front seat is going to zoom up and off they go.

Money cannot buy you love and, more importantly, cannot buy you the loyalty of your employees. Not even at the highest levels. Employees need to feel that the tools for success are there and that the upper echelons of the company will recognize their quest for both personal and professional excellence.

If we were to view your company's employees as weary travelers along the hiring highway, with three or four employees sticking out their thumbs and hitting the road every year and only one or two getting hired to fill those empty slots, how vacant do you think your office is going to look by this time next year?

Or the year after that?

Or five years down the road?

Employee loss is just like those empty corner offices; it creeps up on you, slowly, surely, until one day you look in your rearview mirror to find an empty floor and a company in steep decline because of a dried-up talent pool. The only way to keep those offices full—and your hitchhikers from dusting off their thumbs—is to get to know both of you a whole lot better.

Here is where you start.

Foreword
By Frank G. Risalvato

Each week at my office I receive a blizzard of emails along with dozens of calls ranging from recruiting software vendors, to those seeking some type of endorsement … on through to recruiters calling from other recruiting firms trying to recruit me. If I did not obtain amusement from it all it would be an annoying nuisance.

Most come across amateurish, unprepared, and uninformed at best. They universally fail to grasp my attention or stand out as exemplary in their field from the background noise of the masses that are involved in some form or other within our recruiting and search industries. The majority have failed to invest in themselves yet they would want others to make an investment in them.

As a result, I've become somewhat desensitized to all the claims made by many recruiters. I've also grown justifiably cynical and skeptical when few of those contacting me with the next great idea actually are able to deliver when asked to do so. Even recruiters coming to us for employment fail to follow through when given the chance.

Such is my world when I received a call from Orrick Nepomuceno. When he stated "*I'm writing a book*" and wanted my input. My first thought was "Oh no, Here we go again!"

I was first struck by the unique title. It made me want to open it up and at least start thumbing through the pages to see what the hitchhiker was all about. I then discovered as I read the first two or three chapters, I could not put this book down.

In fact it was entertaining to the point where I wanted to keep reading. I read through page 87 in one sitting. Orrick's abundant use of industry experts and sources which he cites frequently add vast credibility to the concepts he addresses. His use of anecdotes, metaphors, and humor makes it fun to read. And the fact it is all nicely packaged in a "hitchhiker" theme made it enjoyable as well as educational.

Try as hard as I could, I was unable to find any concept or strategy I could disagree with. I could not locate any advice that I have not tried to impart with my own clientele over the years.

This book should be a required reading for every manager whose job relies on hiring others. It is a "must have" for every human resource employee of every company that has at least twelve employees or more and plans to grow through future hiring.

Whether you are a small family owned company, or a Fortune corporation, you will find very valid and valuable advice if you follow just one of Orrick's recommendations outlined in the pages within.

As I look back to extract what lessons could be derived from all those calls and requests of endorsements received at the office that failed to impress me ... maybe, just maybe it all happened for the purpose of appreciating how outstanding the *"Hitchhiker in the Corner Office"* is.

Orrick has proven he is much more than just another recruiter. He is someone who understands the landscape and macro-economics he works in. He is one of those rare recruiters that excels at recruiting and actually bothers to peek up over the office cubicle to see what others in the industry are or are not doing.

I'm confident you will benefit greatly even if you only apply a few of the excellent tips, techniques, and recommendations outlined in the pages that follow.

—Frank G. Risalvato, CPC

Founder of www.searchwizardry.com

Recruiting Industry lecturer, trainer, and author

Introduction:
Curbing the Executive Exodus

Ever feel like there's a hitchhiker in the corner office?

Do you often wonder if that cavalier young executive or leader who never decorated his walls with credentials or degrees is just killing time? Do you ever find yourself showing up a little early in the mornings just to see if that pricey corner office has been cleaned out?

And thinking how you wouldn't be surprised if it was?

If employee retention among your top-level executives and managers is among your biggest concerns, you are not alone. Chris Forman, CEO of AIRS, a training and consulting firm based in Vermont, says, "The labor market is tightening at an alarming rate for high-performing talent. If you're looking for game-changing folks, the slack is all taken up."

Change is in the air and if you haven't felt it yet, you soon will. That change is not hard to see, especially at the top levels. Drake Beam Morin (DBM), a career service firm in New York, finds that CEO turnover "has accelerated at a dizzying pace, with average executive tenure at about three years in the United States ..." Employees are leaving companies at an alarming rate and, even when they *do* stick around for longer than the norm, do not have much retention in today's marketplace.

Another recent study by the consulting firm McKinsey & Co. observes that "... companies are about to be engaged in a war for senior executive talent that will remain a defining characteristic of their competitive landscape for decades to come." The message couldn't be any clearer: hard times are coming and, once they arrive, will be here to stay.

Clearly, the days of twenty-year tenures have gone the way of cheap gas and rotary telephones. These days even your top-level hires can feel more like hitchhikers than loyal recruits committed to buckling up and staying the company course. Oh, their thumbs might be in their pockets today, but let them hear there's a position open in some other company and it's already out, hitching a ride to the next corner office—and the next and the next.

Jennifer Kent writes in *Professional Builder*, "An epidemic is sweeping through the business community … The diagnosis is Retention Deficit Disorder and the symptoms almost always come in the form of turnover of top talent, a declining bottom line and an inability to compete in the marketplace."

Why are so many qualified, talented candidates leaving executive-level positions in such alarming numbers? Challenger, Gray & Christmas, an outplacement consulting organization, finds "a significant increase" in departures at the top levels. Says CEO John A. Challenger, "Higher turnover at the top is the result of increased pressure from shareholders and their representatives on corporate boards."

Additional reason(s) may be more complicated than one might suspect at first blush. Surprisingly enough, it is not because employees are not paid enough. That's right, compensation is *not* one of the top-5 reasons why employees look for greener pastures. What *are* the reasons?

The top-5 reasons top executives leave a company are because:

1. **They want to get closer to "home"** (family matters)

2. **They want more responsibility or a new challenge** (personal development)

3. **They are looking for a promotion** (career advancement)

4. **They have been passed up for promotions** (feelings of inferiority or not enough appreciation)

5. **They feel that their current employer doesn't recognize their efforts** (personal pride)

Regardless of why good employees are leaving, this much is clear: the talent pool is shrinking and there's just not enough water in the pipeline to fill it back up quickly enough. As the boomers are retiring, their jobs are not being phased out. Instead, the retiring boomers are being replaced by younger execs, but there are fewer and fewer among that talent pool to fill these executive roles.

Dunhill Professional Search explains, "Seventy-five percent of executives surveyed said their companies either don't have enough talent or are chronically short of it; ironically, only 10 to 20 percent said improving their talent pool was one of the company's top three priorities."

Meanwhile, according to the Bureau of Labor Statistics, "America is entering a period of economic growth from now through 2012. During this time, employment is expected to increase by 21.3 million, adding about 600,000 more jobs than in the previous decade."

So where's the disconnect? Why are there just as many jobs but only half as many qualified candidates to fill them? Surely there isn't a lack of talent out there, right? Well, yes and no. Yes, there are more than enough lower- to mid-level candidates to staff your restaurants and "make the donuts." The problem is finding enough qualified high-end candidates to line the top tiers of your organization.

How to reverse this trend? Companies need to find the right person first. Filling the slot is vital, but filling it with a qualified candidate versus merely one who just shows up in a nice suit—thumb at the ready—is key to successful recruiting and retention.

Hiring a merely mediocre employee can be costly. Hiring the first available employee instead of the best available can be even more so. How costly? The *Wall Street Journal* reports the total cost of employee turnover ranges from a low of 50% to 60% (The Hay Group) to 100% to 150% (Hewitt Associates) of the employee's yearly salary.

These expenditures include training costs associated with new hires and the price of recruiting efforts required to replace employees. Either way, the costs can be considerable. Factor in the time spent training a new employee and bring he or she up to speed, and you can quickly extrapolate out the collateral costs involved in merely losing one employee, let alone several.

To stop picking up hitchhikers and start hiring some talent that's willing to buckle up and stay the course, employers need to get real about their expectations with employees from day one.

What do you expect? What do they expect? These are not merely touchy-feely questions designed as time-filler during the interview; these are critical issues you both need to explore before ever sitting down in the first place. It is not enough to simply hire someone, expect them to leave after their four-year expiration date is up, and then merely give them a counteroffer to keep them from hitting the road.

A counteroffer will only keep an employee around until the next upwardly-mobile opportunity presents itself. Think of counteroffers as the rest stops along the hiring highway; your hitchhiker might stay in the corner office a little longer, but sooner or later a faster car or bigger front seat is going to zoom up and off they go.

Money cannot buy you love and, more importantly, cannot buy you the loyalty of your employees. Not even at the highest levels. Employees need to feel that the tools for success are there and that the upper echelons of the company will recognize their quest for both personal and professional excellence.

If we were to view your company's employees as weary travelers along the hiring highway, with three or four employees sticking out their thumbs and hitting the road every year and only one or two getting hired to fill those empty slots, how vacant do you think your office is going to look by this time next year?

Or the year after that?

Or five years down the road?

Employee loss is just like those empty corner offices; it creeps up on you, slowly, surely, until one day you look in your rearview mirror to find an empty floor and a company in steep decline because of a dried-up talent pool. The only way to keep those offices full—and your hitchhikers from dusting off their thumbs—is to get to know both of you a whole lot better.

Here is where you start.

The Hitchhiker in the Corner Office is less of a book and more of a journey. It is a voyage through change. It is about looking at your company, your employees, your recruiting policies and your hiring practices differently.

More importantly, it is about looking at *yourself* differently.

How do you view change? An inconvenience? A necessity? A luxury? A nuisance? Whatever your view of change may be, the fact remains clear: change is coming. How you handle the current, looming and ongoing hiring crisis for top-level employees will largely determine the success of your organization.

Still think change is a luxury?

A nuisance?

No matter. I said this book is about change and the first change is how to prepare your organization for the current staffing dilemma. To do so we are going to be looking at your journey through the hiring process like any other journey, full of potholes and rest stops and smooth patches and plenty of hitchhikers posing as ideal candidates.

To keep your eyes on the road and an executive suite full of enthusiastic, productive and most of all loyal employees we are going to have to avoid those potholes that have cost us plenty of freeloading hitchhikers in the past.

Specifically, we are going to avoid the following top-10 hiring potholes:

- **Pothole # 1**: *Hiring as an Event (Versus a Consistent Hiring Philosophy)*

- **Pothole # 2**: *Mistaking Money for True Compensation*

- **Pothole # 3**: *Looking Outward Rather Than Within*

- **Pothole # 4**: *Getting Star Struck Over So-called "Rock Star" Recruits*

- **Pothole # 5**: *Filling Slots Instead of Expectations*

- **Pothole # 6**: *Wasting Those First 90 Days*

- **Pothole # 7**: *Ignoring the New Hire*

- **Pothole # 8**: *Being Afraid of PDA (Public Displays of Affection)*

- **Pothole # 9**: *Foregoing a Recruiter*

- **Pothole # 10**: *Compromising on Excellence*

As an entrepreneur and executive recruiter, I am more than familiar with these potholes. In fact, they have been pointed out to me, time and time again, by my clients who daily decry the hitchhikers who have left their corner offices high and dry and come directly to me to fill them.

But even a new car full of drivers safely buckled in is worthless without a capable driver, so along the way we'll make this a journey of self-exploration as well. Thought-provoking questions and ongoing challenges will make this a highly-interactive process; one designed specifically to keep your employees happy and their thumbs firmly in their pockets!

If you're ready, our first pothole awaits …

Quotes from the Corner Office:

To stop picking up hitchhikers and start hiring some talent that's willing to buckle up and stay the course, employers need to get real about their expectations with employees from day one.

POTHOLE # 1:
HIRING AS AN EVENT
(VERSUS A CONSISTENT
HIRING PHILOSOPHY)

Bump!

Splat!

Bang!

Did you feel that? It's our first pothole down the long and winding road known as the hiring highway, and it's a doozie. But it's good we're getting it out of the way first because **Pothole # 1:** *Hiring as an Event (Versus a Consistent Hiring Philosophy)* is a good analogy for how many of us think about the recruitment process.

And make no mistake; hiring is a process.

It's even more than that; hiring is a philosophy. And not some snooty, academic philosophy you read about in Psych 101 but the true meaning of the word: an attitude, a belief system, a way of life.

In this chapter you will hear a lot about making everyone a recruiter. No, this does not mean your HR department needs to add on another wing or break ground on some new construction. But it *does* mean that the basic job duties of your human resources division—talent searches, recruiting, hiring, retention and relationship-building—should seep out into the rest of your divisions.

Not just one day—not as an event—but every day. This "employee as recruiter" philosophy needs to be ingrained in the daily duties of all employees at all levels. The only way to make hiring a true, sincere *process* is to involve everybody, every day, all the time. If it sounds like so much self-help mumbo jumbo, well, it can't be helped. Change is in the air and nowhere is change needed more specifically than from office to office and cubicle to cubicle.

When hiring is a process, people know about it. More specifically, *your* people know about it. When hiring is a philosophy, your people care about it. Best of all, when hiring is a way of life your people DO it. They do it with you, beside you, behind you and because of you.

Too often we treat hiring like a holiday, crisis, anniversary, emergency, or any other one-time-only, time-sensitive event. Like steam building up until the kettle finally whistles, we only start the recruitment process when some crisis-level talent drain demands a direct and frontal assault. Yet it's just this kind of short-sighted thinking that has us facing a crisis in the first place.

If we want our new hires to buckle up and stay the course, we need to start viewing the hiring process as a marathon versus a sprint. We can't run from office to office and cubicle to cubicle putting out brushfires and making counteroffers and begging, cajoling or threatening our employees to stay put.

Instead, we need to start hiring long before the first interview even takes place. We need to make hiring a priority every day, for everybody. Every employee must be part of the HR department.

The quest for talent should be vigilant and ongoing.

The cost of mediocrity is simply too high.

In this section we will discuss the six basic tenets of making hiring a process, versus an event:

1. **Career Day is Every Day**

2. **Everyone is a Recruiter**

3. **Assessment**

4. **PR is HR (HR is PR)**

5. **Talent Search:** *It's Not Just for American Idol Anymore*

6. **If You Want the Right Person, First Ask the Right Question**

These six key strategies—and, by all means, feel free to add your own—will help to keep us focused on the road ahead versus the recruiter road kill in our rearview mirror. The payoff for having a firm, committed, detailed and specific hiring commitment is increased employee retention, fierce talent loyalty and less hitchhikers along the hiring highway.

Hiring as a process rather than an event is better than some feel good buzz phrase or self-help soft sell. When you take into account the time lost—and money cost—in employee turnover ever year, it's literally money in the bank.

Quotes from the Corner Office:

If we want our new hires to buckle up and stay the course, we need to start viewing the hiring process as a marathon versus a sprint.

CAREER DAY IS EVERY DAY

When did the word "career" go out of vogue? When did it become acceptable to start using words like "job," "gig" or "special engagement" again? Temporary, lightweight words like these—and flighty attitudes to match—are the main reason so many hitchhikers are allowed to get up and go at any given moment. When there is no feeling of permanence or loyalty from the top down, it's certainly not going to be there from the bottom up.

Nothing lasts forever; this much we know. But companies are about more than product; they are about people. Relationships do more than connect us; they enlist us. They involve us, motivate us, reward us and replenish us. There are too many buzz words, throwaway lines and diagrams involved in the hiring process today.

And I should know; it's my business to use them!

But at the end of the day hiring is about one thing: relationships. It's not easy for every executive or manager to know every employee. We all understand that. But every employee must know *you*. Maybe not your favorite color, waist size or home address, but your personality.

Your philosophy.

Your credo and your compassion.

A great example of this is the CEO of the fast food chain Church's chicken, Harsha V. Agadi. I would go so far as to call Mr. Agadi the "poster child" of employee recognition. His reach extends far beyond the corner office. From the front line to the back of the store to the highest levels of his corporate structure, before anyone—*anyone*—is hired at Church's Chicken they are personally interviewed by the company's President and CEO. Even when Mr. Agadi is in Pakistan or India, he'll still take the time to talk to them.

When we treat our own careers like jobs, how can we expect any of our employees to act differently? The first step to avoiding **Pothole # 1:** *Hiring as an Event* is to start with ourselves.

What is a career but a job with permanence?

What is a profession but a career with meaning?

So often we grow casual in our day-to-day lives; to the point of treating careers like jobs and people like employees. When you are in the relationship business, hiring takes on a whole new meaning.

When you hire people instead of employees, every day is career day!

Quotes from the Corner Office:

When there is no feeling of permanence or loyalty from the top down, it's certainly not going to be there from the bottom up.

EVERYONE IS A RECRUITER: 5 *TIPS FOR EMPOWERING YOUR EMPLOYEE TALENT SEARCH*

The days of HR hiring and everyone else firing are over. Nowadays everyone hires; it's just that simple. If you want to stay competitive you must urge your employees—every employee, from the CEO to the entry-level staff—to be on constant alert for finding new talent. Even you are not immune; if you see someone talented, whether they're working for your competitors or waiting on your table or even standing in line next to you at your local bodega, let them know you're looking for good people.

Talent is out there; we just need to find them. Your HR department can only do so much. Clearly, they're not doing enough or you wouldn't be reading this. But it isn't their fault. The idea of having an inactive human resources division—where new hires come to them—is simply old and outdated. Today's progressive companies know that outreach is where it's at; not mere intake.

Some companies even go so far as to dismantle their freestanding HR departments and fold them into the rest of the company, installing recruiters onto every floor and into every division. While this may seem extreme at first, no doubt you can see the eventual benefits of making talent searches a company-wide—versus a division-oriented—endeavor.

As Jeffrey Moses, writing on behalf of *The National Federation of Independent Business*, explains, "When searching for people to promote, take suggestions from other employees. You may not be able to spot the hidden talent under your nose, but employees in the trenches know who has what it takes to move upward in the company."

From this day forward, your employees are no longer exempt from scouring far and wide for your next great hire. Involve them in the recruiting process by letting them know your current needs, growth trends and weak spots. It's not giving away too much information to share honestly and openly with your employees. Instead, it's giving them freedom to make suggestions that could solve your hiring problems overnight.

For your employees to be effective recruiters, they must know not only the need but the deed. In other words, don't just give them the call to action but the action to call on new hires anywhere—and everywhere—they are seen.

Here are five quick tips on how to do just that:

1. **Post internal positions:** Office scuttlebutt is one thing, but you'd be surprised by how many employees truly don't know what positions are open, how much they pay or even their job descriptions. Knowledge is power and to build a powerful recruitment force it takes just a little knowledge to go a long way.

2. **Online access:** Carlson Worldwide (TGI Friday's and Carlson Hotels) does an excellent job of this. But they go the next step by also including online testing in addition to online applications to make sure that they are matching the right talents for the right positions.

3. **Make the introductions:** The HR department shouldn't be cloistered away in some secret recess known only to new hires and those seeking to make an insurance claim. Host a get together or meet and greet where the folks from HR are not only front and center but the honored guests. Attitudes are built from the head down. When top-level execs make hiring a priority, so will everybody else.

4. **Don't send them off empty-handed:** Every employee should have a stack of company literature handy or know the company "elevator speech" for those impromptu talent searches. You never know when they might run into some creative new hire at lunch, around the corner or even on the elevator ride up to the executive suites. Make recruiting easier by preparing them with brochures, packets, business cards and even incentive packages for quick hand-outs to prospective new hires. For instance, every employee at the Ritz-Carlton Hotel Corporation carries a business card. On the back of the card is the company mission statement: "We are ladies and gentlemen serving ladies and gentlemen."

5. **REWARD:** Make sure that your employees are recognized when a new hire they've suggested actually makes the cut. Not everyone believes in monetary rewards but everyone agrees that recognition is a risk-free strategy for keeping employee morale high and the new hire pipeline full. Take your top employee recruiter to lunch, give her a day off, offer him a day of golf at your club. The plusses of rewarding top employee recruiters are well worth the rewards you get in collateral hiring.

Quotes from the Corner Office:

From this day forward, your employees are no longer exempt from scouring far and wide for your next great hire.

ASSESSMENT:
MUCH MORE THAN MULTIPLE CHOICE

It can often be difficult to turn employees into recruiters, and vice versa. Often this is a case of missed messages and lack of communication. Clients often complain that their companies are so rigidly honeycombed, with specific divisions for this and for that, that there's no way to offer hiring advice in a timely and efficient manner.

Likewise, many execs complain that after the pomp and circumstance of the initial hiring push, employees as recruits often drop the ball in favor of lip service and pencil pushing. By openly assessing the employee recruitment program regularly and vocally, you can ensure that everyone is doing their part.

Even you.

Before a new hire is officially on the roster, it can be a good idea to perform various levels of assessment first. Personality and trait assessment testing are on the cutting edge of psychological profiling for potential recruits, and the leader in this field is a company called Wonderlic out of Texas.

Many of these tests will assess a person's personality and character through several tests to measure intellect, leadership and team involvement. Others include handwriting tests.

Many experts agree that personality testing and other forms of assessment offered by companies like Wonderlic can be beneficial to weeding out new hires that might not fit the company mold. Among their primary goals, Wonderlic offers, "Pre-employment screening, employment testing, hiring employees, employee evaluation and workforce development."

The list of tools they offer for assessment are as varied as the companies and CEO's they serve. A smattering of this list includes personality profiles, career directions inventories, interactive skills evaluations and even something called an "entrepreneurial quotient," or EQ test.

Wherever you go to find your various tools for assessment, consider carefully your reasons for doing so. Even the companies who offer such screening processes warn that the tests and measurements are to be used as tools, not "yes" or "no" answers.

Dr. Charles Handler, founder of Rockethire.com, reasons that, "Anyone who follows hiring trends knows that personality measures are gaining popularity as a tool for helping organizations make better hiring decisions. The good news is that decades of research have shown that the use of these tools can have a variety of positive outcomes including reduction in turnover, increased productivity, and better fit between employees and their work environment."

Quotes from the Corner Office:

Before a new hire is officially on the roster, it can be a good idea to perform various levels of assessment first.

PR IS HR
(HR IS PR)

We all know that not all departments are created equally. Every company has a hierarchy. Some divisions more subtly rise to the surface while others proclaim it to the world. How is your company structured? No doubt you can reel off the most important divisions in the space of a minute. Well, if *you* know who rates the highest with you, you can bet your employees can as well.

So where does HR rate? Up at the top or way down below? Companies who treat hiring as an event often treat their HR departments like forlorn children, only called upon when necessary.

One great way to make hiring a priority across the board is to make the HR department more proactive and, for that matter, attractive. Too often companies treat recruiting as if it's airing dirty laundry. Everyone hires. Everyone knows everyone hires. So why not let people know you're always looking for great talent?

A positive spin is a great antidote for the hiring blues. You've got a PR department to make every company press release sing. Why not invest your HR department into turning hiring into a plus rather than a negative by thinking about your own views on hiring differently?

Is your HR department understaffed and undervalued? Is it down a dark and dreary hallway? Secluded and shut-off from the true innards of the rest of the company? While you may not want to physically relocate the entire department, many companies have found that empowering each division of the company with their own HR liaison is one quick way to bring your human resources department more quickly into the fold.

Better yet, when each department has an HR point person, it makes employee recruiting that much easier, quicker and more effective.

Quotes from the Corner Office:

One great way to make hiring a priority across the board is to make the HR department more proactive.

TALENT SEARCH:
IT'S NOT JUST FOR AMERICAN IDOL ANYMORE

If the statistics in my Introduction didn't scare you, I'll reiterate for your reading pleasure: a talent drought is drying up the hiring pool for top-level executives across the country. And the word "drought" is far from hyperbole.

To keep your employee pool nice and full, with plenty of talent in the deep end, I wrap up this chapter on hiring as a process (versus an event) with the suggestion that your talent search be **proactive**, **interactive** and **hyperactive**!

To "actively" elaborate:

- **Proactive:** Hiring will never be a priority to anybody unless it's a priority for everybody. That starts with you. Let your people know how passionate and committed you are about seeking out new talent. Make the hiring process easy and friendly.

- **Interactive:** Make the links in your hiring chain touch every employee, every day in every way. Make hiring a top priority, not an annual event. Start every meeting with the hiring call to arms. End every meeting with a rousing call to action.

- **Hyperactive:** Get busy! Seriously, get busy. Your talent search can never start too early, last too long or involve too many. It may take a little getting used to, but companies who continually stress the hiring buzz and make it an ongoing, daily endeavor are the ones out there snatching up all the talent. If you can't beat them, why not join them?

Quotes from the Corner Office:

Your talent search can never start too early, last too long or involve too many.

IF YOU WANT THE RIGHT PERSON, FIRST ASK THE RIGHT QUESTION

Too often I hear many professionals cry out to me that they have hired the wrong person—*after* they have already hired them. When we finally do get down to the root issue of why they hired this person in the first place, I find out that the hiring authority never asked the right questions when it really counted: from the very beginning.

David Salamme, Human Resources Professional with Sidle Associates, reiterated this when he explained a project for Mohegan Sun Casino in Connecticut. For many years at Mohegan Sun, they hired on a purely gut feeling—with no standardizations or relevant questions to the position. As a result, Mohegan Sun saw a huge turnover.

Sidle Associates helped Mohegan Sun develop standardized tests in order to help the front line hiring authorities develop a clear and focused hiring plan. Instead of hiring on instinct alone, Mohegan Sun now implements behavior and personality testing in conjunction with focused questioning that gets to the heart of the position.

To get to the real personality of the potential candidate you have to ask the tough and loaded questions first off—not after the fact, when it's far too late. Management author and expert Jeff Wuorio explains, "Don't wallow in a snooze-inducing 'Do you work well with others?' spiel. You can interview like an expert—and get the information asked for in a query and 'undercover' feedback that plays a key role in hiring decisions."

Wuorio suggests that you should never let a candidate leave an interview unless you have asked these six strategic questions first:

1. **"If you stayed with your current company, what would be your next move?"**

2. **"What makes you stand out from others?"**

3. **"Tell me your greatest accomplishment."**

4. **"Give me an example of a time when you took the time to share a co-worker's achievement with others."**

5. **"How many hours a week do you need to work to get your job done?"**

6.   **"Do you take enough time to make a decision?"**

Quotes from the Corner Office:

To get to the real personality of the potential candidate you have to ask the tough and loaded questions first off—not after the fact, when it's far too late.

POTHOLE # 2:
MISTAKING MONEY FOR
TRUE COMPENSATION

For decades now, corporate America has relied on three absolute truths:

1. **Death;**

2. **Taxes;**

3. **And a big raise putting a smile on a disgruntled employee's face ...**

Well, two out of three ain't bad. Unfortunately, you can no longer rely on simply throwing money at the problem on Friday and still expect that hitchhiker in the corner office to be sitting there bright and early Monday morning. Why? Well, in addition to the fact that it simply isn't working, it's really, *really* NOT working.

Here's proof: In 2002 the **Families and Work Institute** published the ***National Study of the Changing Workforce***. Research from this groundbreaking study revealed that while *Earnings & Benefits* have on only a **2%** impact on job satisfaction, *Job Quality* and *Workplace Support* have a combined **70%** impact.

These startling results led me to ponder the glaring disconnect between "earnings and benefits," or **money**, and "job quality" and "workplace support," which respondents to the survey clearly considered **true compensation**.

Money.

True compensation.

We have to stop treating the two as apples and apples and more like apples and oranges. Further still, we must come to grips with the fact that apples are so yesterday and oranges are very much in.

This pothole comes second on our journey only because if it came first it might have swallowed up the entire executive level! Seriously, though, this is a major paradigm shift from what most of us—even those of us who are still waiting for the ink to dry on our MBA's—were taught in business school.

So what to do when one of the major foundations of our corporate headquarters is proven to be unfounded, unstable and, worst of all, just plain untrue? Well, in the words of those beleaguered Marines we must "improvise, adapt and overcome."

Here's how:

Quotes from the Corner Office:

Unfortunately, you can no longer rely on simply throwing money at the problem on Friday and still expect that hitchhiker in the corner office to be sitting there bright and early Monday morning.

MONEY CHANGES EVERYTHING:
BUT IT'S NOT EVERYTHING

Say it with me, people: Money is *not* everything.

It's a lot, granted. But it's no longer everything. We need money. The world revolves around money. Money can buy happiness, at least temporarily. Money can provide food, shelter, comfort, entertainment and security.

But then what?

Seriously, after a certain threshold of income is attained—be it $50,000 a year, $500,000 or $5,000,000 per annum—what else is there? A bigger house, a better car, all those CDs you wanted in college but couldn't afford, dinner out a few more times every week, a longer vacation at a better place—and then?

And then?

Today's much sought after hiring recruits are asking "how much?" less and less and "and then?" more and more. New hires know the money will be there. They've studied the flow charts and read the *Wall Street Journal* and subscribe to Monster.com's weekly newsletter. They know who's hiring and who's paying what and for how long and to whom. Information used to be our biggest ally.

Now it's theirs.

The reality is that money no longer makes you unique, special or even all that attractive. Every company is offering money. It's the common denominator, but in today's case it's the *least* common denominator.

That's because there are more of them than there are of you.

Explains Mel Kleiman, president of Humetrics, a Houston-based consultancy, "Most employers now exist in a world of 'negative' unemployment. That means there are more positions available than people qualified to fill them."

In the scramble to snatch up the best first—and keep them around the longest—companies have been forking over large amounts of cash in the hopes of getting to the starting line first. Unfortunately, that's where they stay.

Signing bonuses and higher starting salaries may get the brightest recruits out of the gate, but once they're on board they are no longer a guarantee that shining star won't up and hit the road once the big paychecks wear off.

What employees are looking for today is much more than just the dollars and cents. Some extra perks new hires are demanding include: learning, advancement, emotional rewards, and quality of life.

Let's examine those for just a moment:

- **Learning**: Employees are no longer satisfied with a career; they want a vocation. Something they can be proud of, that contributes to society, that empowers them to feel better about themselves and the work that they do. They want to learn something, both on the job and off. By offering workshops, seminars, added training and even certified coursework in subjects tailored to their job description, employers can offer their employees a sense of educational fulfillment their competitors may be overlooking.

- **Advancement**: There must be a light at the end of the tunnel. Employees are no longer willing to settle for horizontal promotions. To keep from hitting the road they want career advancement; not parallel parking! Just as importantly there must be a timetable in place—and clearly visible. New hires want to know how long it takes the average recruit to move up the corporate ladder. This timetable must be authentic and true. It's not enough to put "five years to middle management" in the corporate brochure and then let the new recruit hear "it's more like eight years" at the water cooler.

- **Emotional rewards**: Work life can't be home life and vice versa, but the workplace must have *some* kind of emotional connection for an employee to feel valued. For an employee to set down roots there must first be fertile soil. This has not always been the case at many of the country's top companies. Emotional rewards include personal recognition, team-building and a more structured sense of the emotional versus the professional. Start with simple things and branch out. A company walk-a-thon for a local charity. Rent out a local movie theater and take in a summer blockbuster. Take front row at a local ballgame. Make your own form of emotional rewards match your company's personality. What would make *you* feel more valued? Start there and go forward. You'll never know what works for you until you try.

- **Quality of life**: Many modern workers, especially those at the corporate level, give big at work. More hours, more duties, more stress, more money, but more is not always better. Sometimes, in fact, *less* is more. We must strive to improve the quality of life at our workplace, in our offices, corporate cafeterias and even in the vending machines in our break rooms. Healthier food, better working conditions, more choices, insurance incentives, flu shots, blood tests, exercise programs, programmed break times and plenty of activities all help to ease the workplace pressure cooker and whip up a better taste in our employees' mouths.

Quotes from the Corner Office:

*Every company is offering money. It's the common denominator, but in today's case it's the **least** common denominator.*

COMPENSATION:
IT ALL STARTS WITH "SEE"

When we redefine the word "compensation" we begin to "see" beyond the limits of dollars and cents and open ourselves to a brighter world of emotional, physical and personal rewards our frustrated employees are craving.

You must look beyond dollars and cents. Synonyms for compensation include reward, reimbursement, payment, and even damages. The common denominator here? Employees want to get paid, just more than in dollars and cents.

Compensation that doesn't appear in your employees' paychecks makes them feel more valuable, special and appreciated. It is the workplace equivalent of the "buy one get one free" attitude that makes us purchase more in the stores or online.

There are many ways to truly compensate your employees that require no money at all and that that don't cost anything beyond some time, thought and a little effort. Some of these include:

- Flexible work schedules

- Casual dress codes

- Achievement awards

- Bonuses

- Interesting and important work assignments

- Tuition reimbursement

- Athletic facilities

- Outside conferences and seminars

- Pets at work

- On-site child care

- Adoption services

- Transportation benefits

- Charitable contribution matches

- Dependent care assistance

- Increasing the amount of work done at home

- Holiday gifts

- Vacation pay and additional vacation time

Even with a minimal outlay from the petty cash drawer, a host of low-cost, high-impact employee rewards open up, such as:

- Pizza Thursdays

- Coffee and bagel Friday mornings

- Regular appreciation dinners or banquets

- Special events like bowling leagues or theme park tickets

Such lists could go on and on, but the point here is to do more, do it often, and do it with forethought, authenticity and careful planning. Not every employee enjoys or is even willing to show up for weekly birthday parties or back-yard barbecues.

In fact, many experts believe that you will not reach everyone. "The number that is thrown around is that, within the business world, 5 percent of the employees at any one given company aren't engaged, they're not interested, and you're not going to ... [get through to] those folks," said Kim Lott, who heads the employee communications section of the Public Relations Society of America.

But my point here is bank on what you know.

Better yet, bank on what you *do*.

If you're in the barbecue biz, blitz that barbecue theme for all it's worth. Have recipe contests and chili cook-offs and potato sack races and Western Wear Wednesdays. Start a weekly cooking show and air it on your own channel.

If you're in the donut business, embrace it. Coffee klatches and holiday donut decorating contests and exclusive recipes just for the corporate office and a host of other quick employee incentives rise to mind.

The corporate culture must be just that; a cultural infusion that spreads from the neck down and reaches into every nook and cranny where life can be breathed and enthusiasm pumped. When a company has a true identity all parts of it match; that includes its employee rewards. And really, have you ever met an employee yet who didn't enjoy a fresh donut and a hot cup of coffee?

Quotes from the Corner Office:

When we redefine the word "compensation" we begin to "see" beyond the limits of dollars and cents and open ourselves to a brighter world of emotional, physical and personal rewards our frustrated employees are craving.

DON'T JUST HAVE AN ATTITUDE OF GRATITUDE; *HAVE AN <u>APTITUDE FOR GRATITUDE</u>*

It is anathema for many CEOs or top-level executives to thank their employees. "Thank them?" I overheard the CEO of a national bakery chain exclaim at a recent convention. "What do you call their paycheck?"

True, he has a point. Employees get paid to provide a service and, once upon a time, that **used to be** enough. But the reality is that paychecks alone are no longer keeping hitchhikers out of the corner office—or off the roads to better opportunities. In fact, many industry analysts see the "paycheck as thank you" syndrome as getting us into this employee exodus in the first place.

So when something's not working we must fix it. Gratitude and recognition are more than just annual events. In the ongoing war known as employee retention, they go a long way toward imprinting loyalty and personality to an otherwise temporary workforce.

Of all the ideas for employee recognition and sincere compensation we've discussed in this chapter, an "attitude of gratitude" is the cheapest, most efficient and hassle-free way to convey a true and sincere sense of employee appreciation.

It takes so little—and yet means so much—to say "thank you," "I appreciate that," or "job well done." For instance, when was the last time you hand wrote a message to an employee to tell them they did a great job? In today's email society, we simply think that we can jet off an email and thank someone for a job well done instead of taking the time to write the message and put it in the mailbox.

Don't just think of it in terms of cost analysis or time constraints. Yes, writing by hand and licking a stamp can be time-consuming. But just imagine the wonder and amazement that employee will feel when he or she receives a thank you note from their boss.

You can't buy that kind of loyalty and retention. Those tiny, seemingly insignificant details have untold rewards that aren't measured in days and weeks of employee loyalty, but years and decades.

But recognition shouldn't always come by remote. A personal handshake, an office visit, even a quick phone call; these can all relay your warmth, sincerity and above all gratitude with an employee—and all in the time it takes to visit the restroom or snag a soda out of the employee break room.

Quotes from the Corner Office:

Those tiny, seemingly insignificant details have untold rewards that aren't measured in days and weeks of employee loyalty, but years and decades.

LEAD? FOLLOW?
WHY NOT DO BOTH?

Over the last decade, powerful leaders have had to contend with the fact that corporations are no longer dictatorships but democracies. There may not be elections or voting booths, but clearly the idea of "servant leadership" is here to stay.

In his foreword to Robert K. Greenleaf's groundbreaking book ***Servant Leadership****: A Journey into the Nature of Legitimate Power and Greatness*, Stephen Covey notes that "the power to cultivate servant-leadership comes from the individual. It's an inside-out approach."

But what does this mean, exactly? To be both boss and servant? To be both leader and follower? To begin, we must recognize that we have always been both leaders *and* followers. After all, we were not born to the corner office. We rose to power, aided by a battalion of teachers, students, mentors, colleagues, coaches, peers, superiors and subordinates.

We do not own leadership; we borrow it. We are but the tip of the spear, the front-line representative of a behind the scenes team of employees who assist us, colleagues who inform us and superiors who aid us.

Was Michael Jordan the leader of the Chicago Bulls during their heyday? Undoubtedly. But no one admits the contribution of his team more than the man himself. "Talent wins games," opined Air Jordan at the pinnacle of his career, "but teamwork and intelligence win championships."

As much as Jordan inspired those who followed him—Kobe and Shaq—he likewise was influenced by his predecessors like Larry Bird and Bill Russell. We, too, are leading a generation of employees based on the inspiration, talent and skill sets passed along to us by our own superiors.

But the servant-leader does not wait for the passing of the guard to hand down those years of wisdom. No, the servant-leader nurtures those in his employ in real-time. Long before Trump brought the word "apprentice" back into vogue, thousands of servant-leaders were "leading" the battle cry to share leadership now, not then.

As executives we should always be on the lookout to nurture and develop talent from within. Consider the CEO of a Fortune 500 fast-food chain that recently took the Senior Marketing VP under his wing.

An unlikely pairing, to be sure. But by fostering an intense relationship of knowledge-sharing and firsthand experience now, this CEO virtually ensures employee loyalty in an almost familial way. It is just this kind of intense servant leadership that turns hitchhikers into drivers of your company's best efforts.

Quotes from the Corner Office:

We do not own leadership; we borrow it.

WIIFM:
My Favorite Radio Station!

WIIFM.

What's In It For Me?

While this may not be a real FM station (or even AM, for that matter) no doubt you and I both hear it all day long.

WIIFM.

What's In It For Me?

We hear it from our colleagues, our customers, our peers and our supervisors. We hear it from our contemporaries, our friends, our co-workers, coaches, mentors and neighbors. Everything we've discussed so far contradicts the What's In It For Me? mantra that runs through most corporate workdays.

But these tools and techniques are not gimmicks or come-ons; they are valuable tools to true and authentic employee retention. They must go to the core of your corporate and personal identity. You have to be sincere about your gratitude to your employees. If you aren't, it will show and come through.

For instance, throwing a pizza party for your team every Thursday is a great way to boost employee morale. But what if you never show up, dig in, and chow down? What if, over time, your prolonged absence becomes clearly conspicuous? What kind of message does that send? Wait, don't answer that. I'll answer it for you:

WIIFM.

What's In It For Me?

If your employees sense that you're just paying lip service to employee retention, anything you do will be less than productive. In fact, it will be counterproductive. You must believe in these practices for them to work. That's not so bad, in the long run. When you genuinely *want* to thank your employees for work well done, it will make all those thank you cards easier and easier to write.

If pizza's not your favorite treat, *offer* your favorite treat. Don't use someone else's template just because it already exists; create your own blueprint for a reward system that works—for you *and* them.

Your employees would gladly rather have a build-your-own-sundae party every Friday—if you've got a sweet tooth—or even a fish fry if that's your weakness. As long as you are there, it makes everything just a little bit sweeter.

The bottom line is that even if these efforts *affect* you, they can't be all *about* you. It must be a partnership, a joint-effort, a servant-leadership scenario so that you are together and not divided. So tune out WIIFM. (It's nothing but noise pollution anyway.)

I've got a new station for you to listen to, playing all the latest HR news and today's hottest employee retention hints: WIIFU.

It stands for What's In It For *Us*?

Quotes from the Corner Office:

You have to be sincere about your gratitude to your employees. If you aren't, it will show and come through.

Pothole # 3:
Looking Outward
Rather Than Within

When it comes to filling empty positions at the corporate level, there are basically two schools of thought: hire from the outside or hire from within. While there are numerous pros and cons for both schools, many companies side heavily on the philosophy that favors hiring from without.

Unfortunately, this becomes our third hiring pothole.

This is not to say that hiring from the outside isn't necessary; it is—and for a variety of legitimate reasons. But it *is* to say that before looking outside of the organization, we should look inward first. Quite often, there are employees already working for you who are more than qualified to fill your current hiring needs.

According to Referenceforbusiness.com, "The advantages to hiring employees from within the company are a greater company knowledge base, continuity, and improved morale." Hiring from within has several other advantages that are often overlooked. These include:

- **Increases employee loyalty**

- **Fosters an internal attitude of collaboration versus competition**

- **Builds drive and motivation among employees**

- **Provides continuity among the corporate mission statement**

- **Eases training time and costs**

What we are trying to create when we work hard to establish an atmosphere of hiring from within is a sense of fierce employee loyalty that makes carpoolers out of hitchhikers. When your workers know that you hire from within, they tend to act accordingly.

Just as important is the fact that an employee who is already familiar with the company will require less time in training and thus be able to begin meeting his or her specific job requirements more quickly and efficiently.

There is also the added side effect of promoting the company's culture or mission statement from within. According to author Stephanie Tuia of the Center for Management and Organization Effectiveness, "When you promote internally, you are hiring people who are already familiar with that work culture and leadership development is enhanced when employees carry on the traditions of a company."

Quotes from the Corner Office:

What we are trying to create when we work hard to establish an atmosphere of hiring from within is a sense of fierce employee loyalty that makes carpoolers out of hitchhikers.

COMMUNICATION IS KEY

Hiring in a vacuum often leads to costly mistakes.

One way to avoid such mistakes is to open the lines of communication from the top down. In other words, we need to communicate our hiring needs, not just to each other, but throughout the company at large. When the entire staff is apprised of a specific hiring need, they can often be your best indicators for who to hire—from the ground up.

Avoid your first instincts to look without. At least, temporarily. Hiring from within doesn't always work out, but in my experience it should be your first line of attack. As reported in Allbusiness.com, "Depending on the size of your business, you can ask the HR department to review the skills and qualifications of people who are already employed by the company to see if there are 'hidden talents' among the staff."

The beauty of looking within your organization first is that the only thing it costs you is time. There are no costly ads to place or booths to set up at job fairs. In fact, depending on your time-pressures for filling the position, this may be an entirely cost-free issue.

What do you gain in return? If you continually seek to hire from within before you hire from without, instead of vice versa, your employees will not only reward you with a much higher percentage of new, qualified hires but, additionally, an added sense of loyalty to their present positions.

And that's a dividend in any business!

Quotes from the Corner Office:

Hiring in a vacuum often leads to costly mistakes.

FOCUS ON THE POSITIVES

When examining the pros and cons of hiring from within versus hiring from without, we can compare them to the advantages and disadvantages of a home-based start-up business versus investing in a franchise.

In the home-based scenario, which we can compare to hiring from within, we already have the existing core of our base of operations in place. Thus start-up costs are lower, time spent building is non-existent, and you invariably start your venture with fatter coffers—and thinner overhead.

On the franchise side, which we can naturally compare to hiring from without, overhead is typically high and rewards are low, especially at first. There is travel time, employee turnover and a host of other unforeseen expenses that make it, if nothing else, a bigger risk than your home-based start-up.

This is not to say that your home-based operation will be more successful than a franchise, but only to urge us to explore our options for hiring from within at least as strongly as our impulse to hire from without.

In short, there are positives to both. In particular, hiring from within saves money, time and effort in a variety of ways. For instance, training time is often reduced thanks to an internal employee's existing familiarity with the organization.

Author Stephanie Tuia from the Center for Management and Organization Effectiveness explains, "Upper-level management positions may require some training, but an internal employee will already have exposure and working knowledge of the company and their position. Their natural leadership development will prosper as they begin to train and educate new employees of the business."

Quotes from the Corner Office:

Upper-level management positions may require some training, but an internal employee will already have exposure and working knowledge of the company and their position.

LESS ORIENTATION + MORE WORK = SMOOTHER TRANSITION

Filling a new position is always a risky proposition. But when hiring from within, there are a host of variables that can at least be identified before making an actual commitment. These include a trusted work record from your own HR department. Merely by having access to work records and fellow employees, you are immediately more familiar with an internal hire versus an external one.

In the following pothole we warn of the dangers of hiring so-called "Rock Star" recruits who look good on paper but don't always stand up to closer, more personal scrutiny. When hiring from within, this danger is greatly reduced if only because your internal employee's "Rock Star" status can be confirmed by, well, other internal employees.

Of course, all of these benefits are dependent upon your employee atmosphere in the first place. Orientation for every employee—new and old—is central to the fostering of company-wide tenets and beliefs.

As reported by Christopher Lai, Director-Head of Business Development, Small Business Services, CSG, American Express International Inc., "If you hire and keep good employees, it is good policy to invest in the development of their skills, so they can increase their productivity. But often, training is considered for new employees only. This is a mistake because ongoing training for current employees helps them adjust to rapidly changing job requirements." [**Source:** Americanexpress.com]

Quotes from the Corner Office:

Merely by having access to work records and fellow employees, you are immediately more familiar with an internal hire versus an external one.

EMPLOYER LOYALTY SENDS A STRONG MESSAGE

We talked earlier in this chapter about communication and I reiterate it here because it is so vital to a company's successful and ongoing recruitment potential. Earlier we talked about verbal communication; this section is about nonverbal communication.

In other words, your actions really do speak louder than words.

It is one thing for employees to hear that your company hires from within, say in your corporate vision statement or even on the walls of the employee break rooms. To witness internal hiring is another matter entirely.

Employees who know the potential for job growth and promotion exist are naturally predisposed to working harder, longer and faster than those who have no such hope in a similar company. It is communication of the non-verbal kind—at its best and at its loudest!

The message of employee loyalty is so loud that you could just find yourself repeating it time and time again. This is not to say that you should have a black and white policy that precludes hiring from without, but only to suggest that when your employees know you look to them first, they're more likely to remain loyal every day, not just during your annual job fair!

Quotes from the Corner Office:

Employees who know the potential for job growth and promotion exist are naturally predisposed to working harder, longer and faster than those who have no such hope in a similar company.

LOYAL EMPLOYEES DON'T HITCHHIKE!

As we round up our discussion of hiring from within versus hiring from without, remember that our ultimate goal is to keep hitchhikers out of the corner office. If you can do that by hiring from within, why not? If, however, the better employee for the job comes to you through outside channels, don't turn your back on him or her without first weighing your options.

Hiring from within is not a failsafe measure or guarantee. Perhaps your organization needs some new blood and it's vitally important to bring in some "fresh meat" to shake things up, view the situation objectively and provide unfiltered advice that may or may not be pleasant to hear. The longer an employer has been around, the less likely they are to be brutally honest.

Fair warning: Hiring from within is not without its drawbacks. Proceed with caution, as you would through any hiring pothole. Explains Donald A. Phin, Employment Practices Liability Consultant Newsletter, "Make sure your company follows a thorough hiring analysis when promoting from within. Promoting solely from within can create inbreeding and stagnate creativity. To guard against these pitfalls, companies should consider filling at least one-third of all positions involving promotions with people from outside the organization."

Quotes from the Corner Office:

Fair warning: *Hiring from within is not without its drawbacks.*

POTHOLE # 4:
GETTING STAR STRUCK
OVER SO-CALLED "ROCK
STAR" RECRUITS

Rock Star recruits are a pothole? Well, not exactly. In fact, Rock Star recruits are the object of this entire book; finding them, courting them, recruiting them, hiring them, training them and retaining them. Unfortunately, in our endless quest for top talent to fill our top positions, we too often get blinded by Rock Star recruits.

We are blinded by their stellar resumes, blinded by their glowing references, blinded by their winning smiles and perfect hair and impeccable pedigrees. In the process, we tend to overlook variables that might come back to haunt us, such as frequent job changes, multiple department switches and feedback that's anything but stellar.

I'm sure you'll agree with me that that IS a pothole.

The problem with Rock Star candidates is that as often as we are looking for them, they are just as busy looking, too. Looking for their next star job, that is. According to HR Alliance, "89% of high performers are always looking for a new or better job, currently looking for such a position or willing to consider another more interesting opportunity."

For this reason, Rock Star applicants are likely to be your biggest hitchhikers. In this chapter we will share how to be on the lookout for ladder climbers, resume-padders and other lackluster recruits that are anything *but* "super."

Quotes from the Corner Office:

The problem with Rock Star candidates is that as often as we are looking for them, they are just as busy looking, too. Looking for their next star job, that is.

What's in a Resume?

Once upon a time when we wanted to buy a book, we walked into a brick and mortar store and combed the shelves. In those days, not so long ago, all we had to go on was the book cover, dust jacket text, and the inherently dubious testimonials from fellow authors. Nowadays, of course, we can peruse Amazon.com and get various unbiased reviews from readers just like us.

It's like a virtual *Consumer Reports* for books!

Wouldn't it be great if we could get the same kind of insider access to that pile of resumes sitting on our desk! Unfortunately, resumes—like book covers—are decidedly one-sided. They are the recruit's interpretation of their best assets, their qualifications and their skill-sets.

I begin this chapter with resumes because to our so-called Rock Star recruits they are our first access to their stellar accomplishments. From that ivy league college to their impressive GPA to a host of recognizable former employees, their resume is a glowing testimonial to all that is "super" about them.

And it very well may be true. But be careful not to judge a book entirely by its cover. Warns Dr. John Sullivan, author of *Rethinking Strategic HR*, "Most of the information we get about candidates is contained in their resume, and most of that information relates to the candidate's skill and experience. While that information can help assess the candidate, it provides no value when it comes to selling the candidate."

In other words, super is as super does. I often witness corporate heavyweights during the hiring process practically gush with excitement about this Rock Star or that, only to caution them that looks can occasionally be deceiving.

That, of course, is why we have the interview process …

Quotes from the Corner Office:

Resumes—like book covers—are decidedly one-sided. They are the recruits' interpretation of their best assets, their qualifications and their skill-sets.

ON THE CORPORATE LADDER, YOU'RE THEIR NEXT RUNG:
READING BETWEEN THE LINES DURING AN INTERVIEW

Please remember that I am not against hiring Rock Star employees. Quite the opposite is true, in fact. However, I *am* against hiring a Rock Star based on his or her resume alone. As with any new hire, do your due diligence and proceed from the glowing resume stage to the sober interview stage. I say "sober" because this is your chance to play devil's advocate and see whether or not your Rock Star wilts—or blossoms—under the pressure.

A resume, like a Glamour Shot, only tells half the story; it's the written equivalent of your recruit's "best side." It is imperative that before you rush into snatching that quality talent off the market you make sure he or she is going to stick around for awhile and not just see your company as yet another rung on his already towering ladder.

Author Dave Ricker of The SearchLogix Group states, "Hiring 'A' talent to fill a B or C level position can be an expensive corporate mistake. Every day, we talk to candidates who say, 'I just took this job to hold me over. Please keep me in mind for any other opportunities.'"

Finally, have a threshold of excellence when it comes to weeding out so-called "A" Players from the rest of the pack. In its "Tips for Making Great Hires" pamphlet series, Coca-Cola lists several attributes that belong to "A" Players. They even begin the section with a great title: *Know What an "A" Player Looks Like*. This puts the emphasis squarely on you. When YOU know what an "A" Player looks like, you'll be able to spot one despite of what his or her resume says.

Don't be pressured into a bidding war over an "A" list player just because he or she is the best thing you've seen lately. Look a little closer, dig a little deeper, and hire the talent from the driver's seat—not riding shotgun. Only a decision made from the seat of power is likely to truly last.

Quotes from the Corner Office:

A resume, like a Glamour Shot, only tells half the story; it's the written equivalent of your recruit's "best side."

If You're Going to Do it, Do it Right

I don't want to leave this chapter without once again singing the praises of Rock Star recruits. Rock Star recruits can add depth, quality and a sense of fervor and commitment to any organization. Unfortunately, when Rock Star recruits are not hired, trained or rewarded properly they have a tendency to do what most superheroes do: fly, fly away!

Just like everything in the workplace, there is a right way and a wrong way to hire the ever-elusive super recruit. Hopefully, I've shown you the wrong way in this chapter. Now I'll call on yet another expert to help me show you the right. According to CareerJournal.com, "Recruiting star performers is more a state of mind than it is the use of any special trick or technique on the Web. The key is to tailor everything you do—job postings and site content—to the unique perspective and motivations of the top talent in the workforce."

Have real expectations; not only from the recruit, but from yourself as well. Because of the tightening job market, I see too many companies overselling themselves and promising career/money expectations they simply cannot keep. Sure, you may get that Rock Star Recruit now, but they won't stay.

Lastly, we should be wary of posting ads that only attract superhero candidates. Ever heard of the saying, "Be careful what you wish for"? Too often we overlook several quality interviewees while holding out for the ultimate, grade-A, superhero, Rock Star elite. But as Allbusiness.com warns, "When recruiting, do not set standards that only a superhero can meet."

Rock Stars are to be courted, groomed and cherished, but not at the expense of quality employees who are the right people for the right job at the right time. With a healthy mix of Rock Stars and team players, any company is setting its sights on a brighter future indeed.

Quotes from the Corner Office:

When Rock Star recruits are not hired, trained or rewarded properly they have a tendency to do what most superheroes do: fly, fly away.

Pothole # 5:
Filling Slots Instead
of Expectations

It is important to have a calm, rational, organization-wide approach to ongoing recruitment and retention. Hiring out of need is like dieting to fit back into last summer's swim trunks; short-term gains without a long-term commitment. Likewise, in the fast-paced world of executive hiring we need to recognize that summer is just around the corner—all year long! We can't treat hiring as a luxury and do it too slowly, nor can we treat it as a race and do it too quickly.

When we hire out of need we are openly asking for the HR gods to frown on us—and do they ever. Pressure hiring puts the pressure in one direction; yours. It also puts the new hire in the driver seat. Not only when it comes to price but other demands as well, such as hours, schedule, vacation time and a variety of perks you might not otherwise be expecting to give.

To avoid filling slots instead of expectations, make your expectations clearer to keep the slots filled in the first place. This involves starting the search process long before you have a position to fill. When you put the emphasis on pre-planning instead of position-filling, you can often take pressure out of the hiring process and have the luxury to do it right the first time.

Will Helmlinger, author of *17 Secrets to Successful Hiring and Retention*, describes the scenario perfectly: "Your natural inclination is to rush, but haste often leads to hiring less than qualified candidates, misinterpreting data, or even skipping critical interview steps. Often quick decisions lead to problems down the road. Avoid 'heat of the moment decisions' you may regret later."

I agree with the author in regard to a well-defined search process. The search really begins with a company making the right decisions on the type of candidate they are looking for first. Then developing position specifications detailing required skill sets, education level, experience and pay scale. This all needs to get done before any resume is looked at. Making the calls, posting resumes and interviewing should be the shortest part of the search process. Do all the work and research ahead of time to save time in the search.

While I prefer to have a calm, rational, organized approach, I caution against swinging too far in the opposite direction and taking too long to hire because you're too afraid to hire quickly. Today, more than ever, there is a "need for speed" in hiring. With the hiring drought amongst us, I often see many companies lose out on the best talent because they take too long to hire someone.

Stay calm, but stay on top of your hiring needs.

Quotes from the Corner Office:

We can't treat hiring as a luxury and do it too slowly, nor can we treat it as a race and do it too quickly.

ACT, DON'T REACT!

To make sure that you are hiring out of speed, not need, it might be helpful to take out your current hiring practices, dust them off and examine them from a new perspective. Ask yourself, "What is holding us back from acting on this candidate? Why is there so much red tape? Why do we have so many cooks in the kitchen? Why can't I simply act on my instincts and hire this kid when I know he/she is the right choice for the job?"

Too often I have watched great candidates get snatched away from Company A because Company B didn't waste time analyzing, re-analyzing and over-analyzing this great recruit; they just hired him! In fact, in my experience, more companies could avoid "Death by Committee" if they simply trusted their instincts more—and their spreadsheets less.

Careful planning *before* the recruiting process is vital to hiring the right person for the right position. Too often, however, hiring committees, peer programs and an outdated, inactive system of internal checks and balances keep good candidates out of the pipeline and in the HR office waiting for an initial interview.

Texas Instruments understands the importance of doing your hiring planning ahead of time. Their strategic leadership team created the "Get the Best" program in 2000, where they developed guiding principles for Texas Instruments leaders to use as a means to excel in the areas of hiring, developing, managing and retaining talent. In Business and Legal Reports (BLR) Best Practices in Recruitment and Retention Report, BLR points out that Texas Instruments' HR team was able to identify five processes for its recruitment strategy:

1. **People Planning.** HR works with the Finance department to help evaluate needs 12 months out. This teamwork between departments helps to ensure that the financial plans of the group will support its hiring plans for the future.

2. **Developing Performance Profiles.** These detailed job descriptions define not only what the candidate needs to accomplish on the job, but what the overall expectations are. There are no surprises.

3. **Centralized Sourcing.** Texas Instruments partners with outside search firms to keep the talent pipeline full, but it also relies heavily on employee referrals. As many as 50 percent of new hires come from employee referrals.

4. **Business Specific Recruiting.** Texas Instruments has several in-house recruiters dedicated to each of its major businesses in the US. This allows Texas Instruments to focus on getting only the best talent.

5. **Assessment and Selection.** The company uses team-based interviews and implements both behavioral questions and technical questions.

Be proactive with new recruits, not reactive. Make time now—don't panic later—and establish protocols for not only making current hires but identifying gaps where they exist to avoid having to fill them so quickly later. It may seem that time spent on hiring when the business is running fine is a waste of that time, but just the opposite is true.

Quotes from the Corner Office:

When we have a firm recruiting and retention policy in place, we don't have to react.

THE INTERVIEW IS JUST A PART OF THE PROCESS (*NOT THE WHOLE*)

We've already discussed the danger of trusting an applicant's resume at face value, but here I take it a step further to include the interview as a mere part of the process, not the whole.

So many in powers of position treat the interview as holy; as if the applicant is on trial and has read an oath to tell the truth, the whole truth and nothing but. While I'm not suggesting that most applicants disregard the truth, I am suggesting they *blur* it from time to time.

The nice thing is, it's for all the right reasons!

As Susan M. Heathfield, the host of About.com's Human Resources division, warns, "During an interview, candidates tell you what they think you want to hear because they want to successfully obtain a job offer. Organizations are smart when they develop several methods for evaluating candidates in addition to the interview."

This is great advice, and a suggestion I readily endorse. What can you do besides the interview to reevaluate a hot prospect? Try these simple ideas:

• **Interview them again:** Call backs are common and, if not abused, can be quite useful in narrowing the field.

• **Role play through several indicative workplace scenarios:** Acting out such scenarios doesn't take much time and can be invaluable in revealing strengths or weaknesses that leap from the resume page and straight to life.

• **Ask questions based on their first interview:** use the first interview as a warm-up to really target specific strengths or weaknesses in the second interview. If time is an issue—for you or the applicant—schedule both interviews on the same day, half an hour to an hour apart.

• **Interview jointly:** Two heads—or even three—are better than one. Ever watch *The Apprentice*? Even the Donald picks the brains of trusted advisors before making the ultimate hire. So should you.

Quotes from the Corner Office:

*While I'm not suggesting that most applicants disregard the truth, I am suggesting they **blur** it from time to time.*

MAKE YOUR WEBSITE A PORTAL, NOT A BILLBOARD

Question: Want better applicants?

Answer: Then build a better website.

While no recruiting measure is ever guaranteed, I can promise you this much: if you build a better website you'll at the very least be heads and tails above a significant portion of your competition. That's because a recent survey by the staffing firm Personnel Group of America, Inc. found that "85% of companies severely under-utilize their corporate web sites for recruiting."

What can a better website do to bring you better recruits? For one, it can be a source of not just your needs but your wants. Information is what separates good websites from bad. When your company establishes itself as one that cares just as much about informing applicants as hiring them, you will start ahead of the pack when it comes to any new hire's job search.

Revamping the human resources side of your website is no mean feat. It can be challenging, time-consuming and expensive. I can tell you, however, that the more aspects of a business's culture and operating philosophy match up, the more cohesive an image you present to future employees.

Think for a minute about the applicant. Chances are he or she first heard about the job online, either through a national, local or classified job search. What's their next step? Checking out your website, no doubt. So if you took great pains to compose a want ad that detailed the job but have a lackluster, non-interactive HR section on your website, how likely is that candidate to be impressed with your cohesiveness?

The best part about making your website applicant-friendly is that, like the other components of a solid hiring rationale, when you make it a firm commitment it becomes easier and easier to maintain over time.

Consult with your webmaster and investigate options for beefing up the "careers," "opportunities," or "human resources" page(s) of your site. Inquire about custom content that includes a variety of HR-related articles, tips for interviewing, protocol and the like.

Even something as simple as enlisting the help of a news-feed site like Feedzilla.com can add targeted and specific relevance to your careers page—and an instant level of respect from tech-savvy, cyber-sophisticated prospective new hires. It may cost a little more, but it's pennies on the dollar compared to the steps each web page takes toward higher employee turnout—and retention.

Quotes from the Corner Office:

Consult with your webmaster and investigate options for beefing up the "careers," "opportunities," or "human resources" page(s) of your site.

CHOICES:
YOURS, NOT THEIRS

Hiring out of need puts you on the receiving end, not the giving end. It is the opposite of taking control because, in effect, you *lose* control. Yes, you are still the one with the job to offer and the authority to give it, but your need is such that your power of choice is diminished and, in some cases, temporarily rescinded.

Too often we hire in a vacuum. We think we have all the time in the world because our company has this, that and the other to offer. However, in this time of thinning candidates and overwhelming need, it is important to keep in mind that each candidate will have as many as three to five other offers from different companies.

It is a buyer's market and, in this case, the buyers are the candidates.

Think about how you typically fill your positions, even those at the top level. Someone hits the road, leaving you in a lurch. If, after a quick search, there is no one internally to fill the slot you must advertise the job and take all comers.

Right?

Wrong.

Nick Corcodilos, from AsktheHeadhunter.com warns, "The traditional recruiting and hiring process is based on a faulty selection model. When you run ads and hold job fairs, you create what's referred to in the research world as 'selection bias'. That is, the process you use biases the outcome of your search for new employees. You get to hire only the people who come along, not those you would like to hire."

Hiring out of need is the pressure play of an unorganized organization. If your corner offices are being emptied one by one, look to the driver, not the hitchhiker. What are you doing—or not doing—that is creating a disconnect between employee loyalty and lack of retention?

If hiring is not a priority for you—now or in the near future—then I'm afraid you will always be hiring out of need and, as a result, always hiring out of need! To avoid this vicious cycle, make hiring a priority now by establish protocols for not only filling your current positions but keeping the pipeline full with prospects for future hires as well.

Quotes from the Corner Office:

It is a buyer's market and, in this case, the buyers are the candidates.

POTHOLE # 6:
WASTING THOSE FIRST 90 DAYS

Time may be of the essence, but just as often it's also in the ether; vanishing into thin air along with our good intentions and long to-do list. Where does our time go? Too often it's spent on too little, too late, and hence we wind up with our tires spinning away deep inside **Pothole # 6:** *Wasting Those First 90 Days*.

The time to think about a new hire's first three months is not halfway through—or on Day 90! It's 90 days *before* their first 90 days. While it's still impossible to go back in time, it's more than possible to look ahead, and that's what we're doing in this chapter.

To recognize the importance of a new hire's mindset, let's step into their shoes for a few paragraphs. Author Michael Watkins, who wrote **The First 90 Days:** *Critical Success Factors for New Leaders at All Levels*, explains of these all-important first three months from inside the corner office, "It's a bit like starting high school; those early impressions, right or wrong, can really stick. And the stakes are high. Failure to create momentum during the first few months guarantees an uphill battle for the rest of their tenure in the job."

It's refreshing to know that your new employee is as concerned about his job performance as you are. But how will concern translate into action? A new hire can only do so much; with support and assistance from you, your team and the HR department, a recently hired employee's first 90 days can go smoothly. Without your valuable support, he or she can sink right into Pothole # 6, practically guaranteeing you've got another potential hitchhiker on your hands.

To avoid losing time, money, energy and yet another new hire to an old competitor, make those first 90 days amazing, rather than agonizing. Like all of our potholes, getting out of this one will require time and effort on your part. But, when done right, the results can truly be amazing.

When done wrong, the costs can be staggering.

According to the Forum Corporation, who actually offers a training product entitled *The First 90 Days*, "As many as 50 percent of outside-hires fail to achieve desired results. Estimates of the direct and indirect costs to a company of a failed hire at the senior-executive level range as high as $2.7 million."

By spending time to create an effective, realistic and repeatable 90-Day Program for all new hires, you do yourself—and them—a great service by meeting both of your needs long before those first three critical months are over.

Quotes from the Corner Office:

Without your valuable support, a new hire can sink right into Pothole # 6, practically guaranteeing you've got another potential hitchhiker on your hands.

FIRST IMPRESSIONS COUNT

All around the country, new hires are happening every day. As with all types of change, how a company treats its new hires during this critical 90-day period varies from boardroom to boardroom. Some make it a priority, others the minority.

Where do you stand?

Regardless of your answer, research indicates that much is riding on—and many are at the mercy of—how you approach this critical timeframe. According to the Forum Corporation, "It is estimated that each year more than half a million managers enter new positions in Fortune 500 companies alone. Whether a manager is hired by a new organization or promoted from within, the organization is often looking to capitalize on the first 3 months of the appointee's experience and so has extremely high expectations of him or her."

To ensure that every new hire is duly impressed with your company's "first impression," take extra steps to make a good one. Here are five simple tips for making your first impression top-notch:

1. **Corner the corner office**: We've all been new hires at one time or another, so we all know there's nothing worse than showing up to little fan fare and even less effort—or having a new hire show up and no one knows to expect him. Once the paperwork is filled out and a new hire walks into that corner office—or corner cubicle, depending—don't leave them stranded. Even if you can't be there personally, make sure someone jazzes up his or her desk with a welcome basket full of first-day goodies like snack foods, office supplies, instant coffee and a paperweight or two. Little things mean a lot, especially in those first few moments inside the corner office.

2. **Send an email greeting**: Create a personalized template that welcomes new hires to the organization and make sure it's the first thing they see when logging in at their desktop computer. Make it short but keep it snazzy; be informative but entertaining. Best of all, be yourself. This simple step can set the tone for a long-lasting relationship.

3. **Food is the universal language**: A simple five-dollar to-go meal can make a priceless impression on new employees when it comes straight from the top. Have it delivered or provide a gift card to the employee cafeteria or some local eatery.

4. **Invitations are inviting**: Send the new employee an invitation to an informal meeting by the end of the week. This lets new hires know you're on the ball and, better yet, lets them know that they should be, too. Many new hires lose that newness by midweek; this way the entire week is a review process that keeps you both aware, enthused and informed. Make the visits positive and upbeat. Says The National Federation of Independent Business, "From day one, ensure that your new hire enjoys a steady diet of encouragement, reinforcement, and coaching. The result will be a strong and healthy employee."

5. **Send them home happy**: Round out that employee's first day with a quick snack or other "parting gift" that sends them home happy. A box of chocolate, a mug and coffee set or a motivational business book; these are all gifts that can be bought in bulk, personalized, and made part of the employee's first day tradition. First days are hard for everyone; make them a little easier by being extra thoughtful—and making an extra-ordinary first impression!

Quotes from the Corner Office:

It is estimated that each year more than half a million managers enter new positions in Fortune 500 companies alone.

TIME IS OF THE ESSENCE

"Time is of the essence."

Nowhere is this truism more accurate than when it comes to those crucial first three months in a new hire's lifespan. As author Michael Watkins explains in his book *The First 90 Days*, "The president of the United States gets 100 days to prove himself. You, however, get 90. In today's competitive business climate, the six-month honeymoon is over."

How high are your expectations for new hires? Let me rephrase that question: How high are your expectations for *yourself?* After all, the leader takes the lead and all others follow. When you make those first 90 days a priority, others will as well.

Start from the beginning. Create a first-day orientation that makes an event out of an otherwise non-event. This can be with an HR rep, a colleague or a mid-level manager. The duration can be short—from half-an-hour to half-a-day—but the impact will be big when see through a new hire's eyes.

Afterward, establish objectives from that day forward that express your interest in—and expectations of—your new employee. These can be insignificant, such as a weekly "meet and greet" for a few minutes every Friday or a quick check-up in the new hire's corner office. Every month, make it a priority to monitor the employee's progress—then do it.

Not sure how?

No worries; just S.E.E. my next section:

Quotes from the Corner Office:

When you make those first 90 days a priority, others will as well.

S.E.E. RESULTS WITH THIS PROVEN SYSTEM OF *SATISFACTORY EMPLOYEE EVALUATION*

With time on the line, it's critical that you be able to evaluate an employee's performance regularly and accurately. Asking a new hire "how they're doing" is about as accurate as asking your spouse how they liked that new bathrobe or tube of car wax you gave them last Christmas.

Every company will do what it feels right and fruitful for themselves—and the recruit. My guidelines are just that; mere guidelines. Personalization and prioritization are the twin pillars of adapting guidelines into policies. Over time you will adjust and adapt them to fit your specific needs—in your specific timeline. While the methods may differ for each company, follow-through is a universal truth for all companies.

In other words, whatever you do, be thoughtful and do what you say you are going to do. Follow-through; stick to it. If you say you are going to have monthly progress meetings with every new hire, you better hold yourself to sticking with it. Otherwise, you will lose credibility with the new hire.

To secure **S**atisfactory **E**mployee **E**valuation (which also just happens to turn out to be "SEE") I've come up with the S.E.E. Method:

- **Set a Timeline**: 90 days will come and go before you know it if you don't set specific guidelines for evaluation along the way. To make it easy on yourself, schedule an evaluation for the end of each month. This gives you three evaluations—one for each 30-day period—and plenty of time to offer much-needed feedback along the way.

- **Evaluate Their Progress**: Establish a routine manner of evaluating a new hire's performance. Many of my clients prefer a combination of existing materials—such as questionnaires and performance appraisals from superiors—and personal touches such as face-to-face time, workshops or even shadowing opportunities.

- **Ensure They Receive Feedback**: Feedback is critical and must flow both ways. As author Susan Hoy writes in *Chiropractic Economics*, "Allow your team to communicate with you without fear of reprisal. Sensitive issues must be worked out with sensitivity. Insist on two-way communication."

Quotes from the Corner Office:

Asking a new hire "how they're doing" is about as accurate as asking your spouse how they liked that new bathrobe or tube of car wax you gave them last Christmas.

TAKE THE JOURNEY TOGETHER

Make sure that you participate before, during and after the hiring process; that includes this critical 90-day period. There is no simpler impact you can make on any employee—new or old, hitchhiker or carpooler—than by your mere presence.

It's called Management by Walking Around, or MBWO and, according to John Reh, About.com's Management Guru, it "… really does work. Not only are people more apt to approach you in 'their territory,' but you will hear and see things that never make it into the reports that come into your office. Besides, when your employees see you walking around, they begin to see you as a person, not just as 'the boss.' It's a lot easier to mistrust 'the boss' than to mistrust an individual."

This policy extends to every new employee, sure, but also to your other employees as well. You can start this healthy habit by making the new hire your new priority. It doesn't take much; a simple pop-in once or twice a week, at first, is all that's necessary to show your presence—and support.

Later the visits can become less frequent, but more impactful. As time permits, schedule brief but relevant visits to review policies or performance. I recognize time is limited but so, too, is it valuable. Remember our statistics from earlier in the chapter and the staggering costs of new hires that hitchhike. The time it takes you to invest in every new hire could just mean the difference between turning them into an asset—or a liability.

I'll end this section with a quote from Howard Cowan in *Managers Magazine*, who sums up my sentiments exactly with the words, "Our recruiting success can be attributed to many things, but most importantly to the fact that I treat the recruiting process the same way that I treat any sales process. We set goals, and we map out plans to reach those goals. We constantly monitor the plan and our goals, and we are willing to adjust or change plans as needed to set us back on course."

Quotes from the Corner Office:

When your employees see you walking around, they begin to see you as a person, not just as "the boss."

POTHOLE # 7:
IGNORING THE NEW HIRE

What to do *after* the first 90 days? Every leader's answer is different, but this much is clear: interrupting that successful momentum of those first three months is guaranteed to send mixed messages to a happy employee.

And happy employees don't hitchhike.

If it sounds like I'm suggesting you baby your new employees, that's because I am; new hires, like newborns, need "proper care and feeding." And I'm not alone. In fact, the National Federation of Independent Business agrees whole-heartedly, "In some ways your new hire is like a newborn——fascinated by this exciting new world but in need of care and guidance."

It's up to us to give our employees "proper care and feeding." That's why **Pothole # 7** is *Ignoring the New Hire*. I know what most of you are thinking: "I'd never do that." (But you would be surprised at how many companies I see doing this very thing!) I suppose it's human nature; everyone's definition of "ignore" is different. For some leaders, ignoring a new hire might mean passing them in the hall without acknowledgement or forgetting to update them about the upcoming employee picnic. For others, it can mean forgetting their name or to process their paperwork.

The result is the same: you are perceived as poor on follow-through and, worse, as someone they might not want to "follow" in the first place! Don't ignore your new hires; go the opposite direction. Celebrate, recognize and embrace them in ways that are obvious and rewarding.

This chapter contains some great ways to do just that.

Quotes from the Corner Office:

If it sounds like I'm suggesting you baby your new employees, that's because I am; new hires, like newborns, need "proper care and feeding."

USE THE BUDDY SYSTEM

Like shiny new pennies, if you're not careful, "shiny new employees" can often slip through the cracks. Much time, research and effort has been put into researching the reasons why new hires hitchhike versus stick around, but you can save yourself the trouble by following a much simpler rule for employee retention, this one courtesy of America's kindergarten teachers: use the buddy system.

Al Trellis, a co-founder of Home Builders Network, explains, "It is crucial that a new individual understand the particular management systems and culture of the company before jumping feet first into managing a full schedule. The easiest way to do that is to let him work under the supervision of someone who is familiar with the systems and culture."

While you should clearly establish yourself as a leader, mentor, colleague and co-worker, share the burden of not ignoring new hires by automatically assigning them a "buddy." This should be a colleague in the same department, preferably a co-worker rather than a supervisor.

At Hunter Douglas, a leading manufacturer of custom widow coverings headquartered in Saddle River, New Jersey they take the "buddy system" to the next level. Hunter Douglas implemented a mentoring program in 2000 to foster good employee relations. Betty Lou Smith, Vice President and founder of the corporate HR function at Hunter Douglas, explains, "It's very stressful when an employee begins a new job, and anything that you can do to make it more palatable is helpful."

Under this system, long-term employees mentor and work with new employees to adjust to the company culture, norms and daily work responsibilities which range from where the break rooms are located and how to access necessary work supplies to the social norms such as employee introductions.

The rewards of the buddy system are many; the drawbacks few. In particular, the buddy system:

- **Creates camaraderie**: no matter how outgoing your new hires may be, they can always benefit from a little one-on-one relationship-building. Assigning them a buddy quickly gives them a contact person, "go to" pal and, quite possibly, a new friend. None of these are liabilities; all are assets.

- **Empowers ambassadors**: When choosing your buddies, or instructing HR on best buddy assets, make sure you're on the lookout for employees who need a boost themselves. By helping others, we often help ourselves; by helping new hires, we often help reenergize our own employee commitments.

- **Maximizes efficiency**: When current employees buddy with new hires it makes them both more efficient. The new hire "learns the ropes" more quickly thanks to the one-on-one access and, collaterally, the "buddy" prospers by reevaluating his or her own loyalty to the company line.

- **Shares responsibility**: your plate is full enough without being every new hire's buddy. When employees share in the responsibility, they act as your representative and you are showing them respect by assigning them the position. While many employees will see this role as an added burden, at first, in time the "buddy system" will prove to be beneficial to all.

Quotes from the Corner Office:

Like shiny new pennies, if you're not careful, shiny new employees can often slip through the cracks.

FEEDBACK ALA NIKE: *"JUST GIVE IT!"*

Honest, timely and consistent feedback is vital in fostering an atmosphere of trust and two-way communication for your new hire. He or she is often disoriented and eager to please; not always a winning combination. New hires often think it's best to avoid communicating with the boss, if not out of outright fear than at least out of fear of not knowing proper protocol.

Some leaders have an open door policy; others expect employees to "speak only when spoken to." Which one are you? If you're not quite sure, the National Federation of Independent Business has a suggestion: "Set up a one-to-one orientation. Be sure your new employee clearly understands your policies, practices and traditions——and take the time to carefully explain anything he or she doesn't understand."

Feedback can come in many forms:

- **Face to Face**: If time permits, meet face to face with the new hire when giving feedback. This is always the most effective. But most of all be a good listener. Pay attention to your employees. Sounds simple, but it is usually very difficult for most of us. Says Maureen Dolan Rosen, a human resources expert based in Chapel Hill, N.C., "Among the things I stress in workshops with managers is 'learning how to listen better'." She'll also offer a story about one of her former bosses, who cleverly perched his hand under his chin in meetings and appeared to be listening intently to whoever was speaking. But if you looked closely, under his glasses, his eyes were closed. He'd use the meetings to snooze.

- **Electronic**: When done properly, email from the boss can be just as good as a meet and greet. As such, it has become an important communication tool today. But understand the nature of the message and recognize that email is not a universal solution for all problems. The most delicate of situations are always best handled face to face—or at least on the phone. Email is never appropriate when emotions are at play and definitely not when someone is getting laid off. (Yes, I know it happens, but don't rely on it.)

- **Written**: Employee reviews should always bear the imprint, if not the actual handwriting, of the company leader.

- **Singular**: You or your representative can provide the feedback one-on-one.

- **Committee**: You and a group of colleagues can provide the feedback by committee or in an informal, round table discussion.

Whichever form you choose, be consistent, timely and honest. By no means am I suggesting that the hiring drought has gotten so bad that you should keep a lackluster, mediocre or even ho-hum employee. Honest, timely and consistent feedback will assure that good employees get better—and bad ones get the message!

Most of all keep it consistent and don't have surprises at the annual recap or evaluation. You will lose credibility with a potential hitchhiker if you come "loaded for bear," as they say, and layout all their shortcomings in a one-time meeting.

The annual evaluation should be more about recapping what you have discussed throughout the year and how to keep improving. Keep your message consistent. Know your values and how you want to be perceived. If you are sending mixed messages, explain them—or suffer the consequences.

Quotes from the Corner Office:

Honest, timely and consistent feedback is vital in fostering an atmosphere of trust and two-way communication for your new hire.

THE RECOGNITION MISSION

How do you fare with employee recognition? Is it a once-a-year affair or once-daily? The answer will be a personal one, of course, but far from unimportant. As Rich Castro writes in the *Realty Times*, "As the leader, what inspires you besides the money and the stuff? Create that vision in your company. What really inspires most people is that you notice them … that you care about them. And most of all, recognize them … not for their production, but for being themselves."

The best part about recognition is that it IS personal; it should come from the heart, not the *Employee Retention Manifesto*. It can also be inexpensive, simple, effortless—and downright painless. Here are four simple rules to follow when offering recognition to new hires:

1. **Make it obvious**: Feedback may be personal, but don't give it in some secret code. Make sure the employee knows he or she is being recognized. This can be obvious to them only, in some kind of private ceremony, or obvious to the company, through public recognition.

2. **Make it personal**: Automation makes life easier, particularly when it comes to the workplace. But don't set your Recognition Mission on auto-pilot. It's okay to buy gifts, cards or even certificates in bulk, but make sure you personalize them in some manner that says more than just "we appreciate _____."

3. **Make it regular**: Employee recognition should be standard fare around the workplace, and not just for new hires. Simple events like employee picnics add togetherness to any company routine, but even minor treats like complimentary coffee and donuts in the break room every Friday morning not only keeps employees fed, but mindful of who's doing the feeding!

4. **Make it creative:** Creative acts of appreciation can be as simple or as elaborate as need be—as long as they are original, inspired or resourceful. Don't send a "thank you" card; send a "thank you" cookie or, better yet, a pizza with "thank you" spelled out in pepperoni. Never give an empty mug; fill it with something fun or tasty, like chocolate pencils or gummy candies shaped like office supplies.

Whatever you do, be it **obvious**, **personal**, **timely** or **creative**—but hopefully a combination of all four—it has to be honest and meaningful. Otherwise, you might as well not do it at all.

Quotes from the Corner Office:

*The best part about recognition is that it IS personal; it should come from the heart, not the **Employee Retention Manifesto**.*

WANT TO KEEP THAT CORNER OFFICE FILLED? *PAY LESS MONEY AND MORE ATTENTION!*

Am I serious? Pay less money? And more attention? Well, the "less money" part is up in the air, but the "more attention" part certainly isn't. As Jennifer Kent writes in *Professional Builder*, "Employers must … understand that they will need to pay an increasing amount of attention to their employees, offering them more than a paycheck. They'll need to design good jobs and entice high performers with a vision that they can embrace. Those employees worth retaining want a stake in building a better company, of becoming part of something bigger than themselves."

Feedback, recognition and attention are the cornerstones of keeping employees in the corner office. They provide more than mere back-patting and praise-giving, they provide actual evidence that their employer cares, shares and is aware of them, their performance and their value to the company.

Ms. Kent's quote reinforces what I stated earlier in the Introduction to this book: Compensation is *not* one of the top-5 reasons why employees look for greener pastures. Fortunately, more attention is.

Make time for your employees. Regular one-on-one meetings are important. If the employee works remotely, schedule at least two meetings a month. Monte Enbysk, a lead editor for the Microsoft.com network, says, "Talk about their career paths and how you envision them growing in their jobs. On the flip side, employees need to be aware of bosses' time pressures. And don't take phone calls during meetings, unless it is an emergency. Show your employees they have your full attention."

The T.G.I. Friday's chain of restaurants has a great philosophy for providing employees with just the type of recognition and fun you'd come to expect from this successful franchise. In the annual *Spirit of the Industry 2006* report presented by the National Restaurant Association Educational Foundation, Nation's Restaurant News and The Cocoa-Cola Company, it states, "Anyone who has ever visited a T.G.I. Fridays … knows … having fun is a part of their culture. This fun does not stop at the end of the work day, either; their employees are provided with fun and exciting programs, letting them know how crucial they are to the success of the organization."

Quotes from the Corner Office:

Those employees worth retaining want a stake in building a better company, of becoming part of something bigger than themselves.

POTHOLE # 8:
BEING AFRAID OF PDA
(PUBLIC DISPLAYS OF
AFFECTION)

There's an old truism veteran teachers all across the country offer to rookie teachers the first day of every new school year: "Don't smile until December." This smile-free strategy might have worked a whole lot better back in the 1950s, when I suspect the truism rang a lot "truer," but few teachers take this old chestnut seriously anymore.

Unfortunately, far too many business leaders *do*. In fact, Public Displays of Affection (or PDA's, as they're more "affectionately" known), have been frowned upon for so long it's hard to take them seriously. But take them seriously we must, because PDA's are making a comeback—and it couldn't happen at a better time.

According to Susan M. Heathfield, About.com's Human Resources Guru, "When you recognize people effectively, you reinforce, with your chosen means of recognition, the actions and behaviors you most want to see people repeat. An effective employee recognition system is simple, immediate, and powerfully reinforcing."

To truly recognize the value of a PDA, let's break it down, shall we:

- **Public**: In plain sight, where everyone can see and appreciate it. If an award is presented behind closed doors with only a few people, did it really happen? Showing appreciation means nothing if you don't share it with others. I don't mean small awards, but things that really help to improve a company. If it is important for your company and culture, let everyone know about it.

- **Display**: A way of turning consideration into a presentation. To turn daily PDAs into displays, just think outside the box—or at least outside the office. Pause for the last 15 minutes of the day and announce a list of a few names, or just one, for boasting a job well done. Take a casual office thanks and turn it into a display by seeking out the employee in question in the break room, cafeteria or even by the water cooler.

- **Affection**: Fondness, warmth and friendliness. Be sincere. Next to saying, "I'm sorry," one of the hardest things for anyone to do is give someone praise. Learn how to do it now. If you can't give praise, you will lose credibility with your employees and they will only perceive you as someone who brings only negatives. Be truthful and honest.

Not so hard, is it? On their own, each of the PDA's letters makes perfect sense. So why is it so difficult for so many of us to put them all together? In an effort to make the workplace a lot more effective—and hire far less hitchhikers—I present **Pothole # 8**: *Being Afraid of PDA*. But fear not, the many valuable benefits of PDA are just a few paragraphs away!

Quotes from the Corner Office:

An effective employee recognition system is simple, immediate, and powerfully reinforcing.

KEEP 'EM COMING BACK FOR MORE

Public Displays of Affection are no longer voluntary; they're mandatory. That is, if you want to avoid hitchhikers in the corner office. According to Gregory Smith, author of *Tips 'N Techniques: Dynamic Ways to Reward, Energize & Motivate Your Team*, "People have a basic human need to feel appreciated and to be recognized. If you don't give them that, they will seek it out elsewhere."

In trying to explain why so many executive-level employees stick their thumbs out after only a few years (3.5, to be exact, according to the Bureau of Labor Statistics), Mr. Smith does an eloquent job of boiling it all down for us. In short, if we don't do it, someone else will. And if someone else will—and we won't—hitchhikers will always be our problem, not theirs.

PDA's can range from simple employee gifts to gift cards to greeting cards to personal greetings to personal messages to messages of inspiration to inspirational music to music CDs to CD-ROMs to, well, just about anything. They can be singular or collective, simple or elaborate, personal or private.

The trick is to understand that it's not the actual PDA that counts, but that we give one in the first place. Employees aren't very specific about what they want to be recognized with, but they're very specific about wanting to be recognized.

If we want to retain the best, we have to give them what they want—especially when it's in our power to (easily) do so. PDA's are definitely in our power. They don't have to be significantly expensive or significantly taxing; they just have to be significant.

In *The 24-Carrot Manager* by Adrian Gostick and Chester Elton, they list a variety of "Once-a-week carrots" to "praise effort" and "reward results," including: "box of chocolate bars, half-day off to spend w/kids and tickets to movie, play, game." To help you explore your creative side, I've expanded on their list with some specific, timely and knock-out gifts that say "I appreciate you" in ways you never dreamed possible.

Nothing on this list is intended to be written in stone, but merely a guide to express how creative, rewarding and memorable PDA's can be—if only you'll make them a priority:

- **Personalized Golf Balls.** www.mortongolfsales.com. Take your gratitude to the golf course and personalize a dozen Titleists for that special employee.

- **"Thank You" Cookies.** www.deananddeluca.com. Offered by Dean & Deluca and baked by Eleni's New York, your outstanding employee will receive 18 colorful, hand-decorated butter cookies adorned with a festive "Thank You."

- **Grand Slam Message.** Various stadiums and arenas offer this great way to make a very public show of appreciation for the sports fans in your office. Take the team out to a ball game and have your message on the JumboTron at the 7th Inning Stretch. At Fenway Park in Boston, all that is required is a donation to the Red Sox Foundation.

- **Message on a Bottle.** www.bottleyourbrand.com. Customize a wine label that shows your appreciation, then shop for a wine varietal that is worthy of the occasion.

Quotes from the Corner Office:

If we want to retain the best, we have to give them what they want—especially when it's in our power to (easily) do so.

LESS IS MORE, MORE OR LESS

There's a reason PDA's only have three letters: less is more. According to Topresults.com, "Nothing elaborate is required. Simply spending time together with the opportunity to say thanks and to exchange ideas is valuable."

Value is in the eye of the beholder, and in this case your beholder is a tentative new hire eager to find his or her way straight into that corner office. Help your new employees by showing them that not only is kindness contagious, it's downright unavoidable.

When we share genuine, unambiguous compassion with our coworkers, colleagues and especially our new hires, we make the transition from outsider to insider smoother for all of us. Smoother transitions translate into longer durations and, eventually, higher employee retention.

And isn't that what it's all about?

When you get right down to it, what is affection but another word for love? Don't be the kind of leader who thinks loving his employees, his work or his passion makes him any less of a leader; it doesn't.

If anything, the opposite is true. While giving a keynote presentation for The Coffee Bean & Tea Leaf Company recently, Ken Blanchard, author of *The Simple Truths of Service*, expressed his feelings on love. Blanchard explained to a room full of leaders that "… leadership is about love; loving their mission, their customers, their Team Members and, finally, loving themselves enough to move out of the way so others can shine. It is this model of leadership that will inspire Team Members to provide memorable service!"

Quotes from the Corner Office:

Help your new employees by showing them that not only is kindness contagious, it's downright unavoidable.

A P.D.A. A DAY KEEPS HITCHHIKERS AT BAY!

If you need more convincing that Public Displays of Affection are more important than ever, consider this: Corpnote.com, an innovative company specializing in employee appreciation cards explains, "Showing your employees you recognize and appreciate their dedication and hard work is one of the most important motivation strategies in today's workplace. And it doesn't take expensive gifts or paid time off to reward your staff."

In honor of our five-day work week, here are five great ideas for making PDA's a piece of cake:

- **Monday**: Start the week off on the right foot by starting the week off on the right foot—literally! Instead of getting straight to work, get straight into shape with a Monday Morning Walkathon.

- **Tuesday**: So what if there are still four work days left? Make them all the more valuable with a simple Tuesday Treat. It can be muffins in the break room or mints on their mouse pad or an extra half-hour at lunch. By continuing the weeklong festivities with something everyone can look forward to every Tuesday, you're well on your way to making PDA's, not to mention weekdays, practically pain-free.

- **Wednesday**: Make midweek the best part of the week by instituting Midweek Madness. Skip lunch and throw an employee appreciation party every Wednesday from noon to one. Cater the affair cheaply and casually and offer door prizes or raffle tickets.

- **Thursday**: Start the weekend mode a day early when you invite the ice cream man to your door. Schedule weekly delivery of inexpensive but tasty treats from the local ice cream truck and watch the employee parking lot flood with grateful co-workers new *and* old.

- **Friday**: Kick off the weekend with a corporate pep rally to show your appreciation and support. It can be scheduled for the last half-hour of every Friday and filled with low-key but high-impact company closeness.

Quotes from the Corner Office:

Showing your employees you recognize and appreciate their dedication and hard work is one of the most important motivation strategies in today's workplace.

USE THE 3-C METHOD:
CREATIVITY, COMFORT AND COMPASSION

Creativity counts. Don Jacobson of Govleaders.org echoes this sentiment when he writes, "Every employee has a need for praise and recognition, and the more often they get it the better. Supervisors are in the best position to give recognition, but few do it often enough—or creatively enough."

By using the 3-C Method, we ensure that we cover the basic foundation of making our PDA's full of Creativity, Comfort and Compassion. Why only 3 C's instead of, say, 13 or 30 or even 300? Well, as we discovered in the last section, "Less is More."

In other words, the less hassle a PDA is for YOU, the more likely you're going to be to give one out. The best part is, the 3-C Method is very simple to remember—Creativity, Comfort and Compassion—and even easier to implement:

- **Creativity**: Don't do what everyone else is doing; do what no one else is doing. Put yourself in a new hire's shoes and ask yourself, "What would a PDA look like to me?" Now take your answer and turn it upside town, look at it again, and see what else shakes loose. If everyone else is offering pizza on Fridays, offer "make your own pizza" on Fridays. If everyone else is installing a cappuccino machine in their break room, start a flavored cappuccino tasting day.

- **Comfort**: If your company is small, keep your PDA's within limits. What works for some huge conglomerate might not work for you. Conversely, if you run a large company, think BIG. What works for nine employees doesn't always work for 90—or 900. No PDA should ever be uncomfortable to give—or receive. The more appropriate you make it for you, your company and your employees, the more comfortable everyone will be.

- **Compassion**: The key ingredient to every PDA is "Affection." What is affection if not compassion? Think again of what it felt like to be newly-hired, once upon a time. Most of us didn't seek anything more than a compassionate word from a colleague or coworker to keep our spirits up and our wanderlust down. The sooner you tap into your compassion, the easier it will be to start giving out PDA's ASAP.

Quotes from the Corner Office:

The less hassle a PDA is for YOU, the more likely you're going to be to give one out.

POTHOLE # 9:
FOREGOING A RECRUITER

I'm here to tell you that hiring a recruiter is NOT a last-ditch effort. And by making it **Pothole # 9** I am in no way ranking this step as lower in importance than our first eight potholes. The fact is recruiters make life easier; for the employer and for the potential employees.

According to ProfessionalResumes.com, "In today's competitive job market, there are some definite advantages to using a recruitment firm. Both job seekers and hiring companies can benefit from the services offered by a professional recruiter. The advantages to each party, though, are somewhat different because they come to a recruiter for different reasons and with different perspectives."

How can a recruiter help you? Let's start by asking a more direct question: How can hiring a recruiter help a new employee help you? Awkward question, simple answer: The potential employee comes to a recruiter to make his or her job search easier. The recruiter does this by targeting each new recruit with specific openings in his personal database of jobs, employers and opportunities.

We ask again, how can a recruiter help you? When a recruiter knows your specific needs, specifications, corporate philosophy and culture he is more likely to bring you qualified candidates who fit those needs, specifications and corporate philosophy. Recruiters are like professional matchmakers; only happy when a union goes smoothly. When a match goes wrong, nobody's happy. Not the recruiter, not the recruit and especially not the employer.

When the employer is happy, the recruiter is happy. Therefore it follows that a recruiter's job, first and foremost, is to make the employer happy. He achieves that prime directive by bringing in only the best and the brightest.

More importantly, view a recruiter as a specialized agent of your company, but one that can dig in deeper than your company may be equipped to do. Most successful recruiters talk to approximately 30—50 people a day—to clients and candidates alike. The more niche a firm, the more they are apt to know the pulse of your industry and know what is going on with your direct competition. Knowing what your competition is up to is always a good thing.

As Sun Tzu counseled in *The Art of War*, "Know thy enemy."

Recruiters aren't for everybody, but they could just be for you. Before you turn your nose up at enlisting the aid of a professionally-trained, well-connected recruiter, let's clear up some of the confusion and make the roadway a lot clearer so that you can avoid this particular pothole.

Quotes from the Corner Office:

The fact is recruiters make life easier; for the employer and for the potential employees.

CLEARING UP THE CONFUSION
(*BEFORE GETTING DOWN TO BUSINESS*)

There's no doubt that a world of confusion surrounds the lucrative field of professional recruiting. But don't let confusion cost you a single qualified recruit. As Robert L. Pearson, chairman and chief executive officer of Pearson Partners International Inc., an executive-search firm in Dallas, puts it, "Confusion about how recruiters operate has put many a career at a disadvantage."

Recruiters are only as good as the companies who hire them and the recruits they place. Successful recruiters don't get that way by burning their employers. Successful recruiters only succeed when the recruits they bring are worthy of the employer they bring them to. This simple equation of **qualified recruit + savvy recruiter = happy employer** makes you the sole beneficiary of a recruiter's hard won efforts.

Only when talented employees meet eager employers does a recruiter earn his pay. And who, exactly, pays the recruiter for his services? The employer does. So who is the recruiter going to look out for?

You, the employer, of course.

Few of us are looking to incur extra costs, especially when it comes to the already-costly hiring process. But even less of us can pass up a good investment, and recruiters are a good investment of your valuable time.

By targeting quality recruits for your executive positions, they decrease turnover and increase retention. Recruiters also add time value. Remember that time is of the essence when it comes to hiring. In addition to going deeper than most HR departments are willing to venture, recruiters can get in faster, often into areas where most companies fear to tread, to find the best talent.

Not a bad investment, indeed.

Quotes from the Corner Office:

Recruiters are only as good as the companies who hire them and the recruits they place.

SEARCH FIRMS AS SEARCH FILTERS

In a world of tense competition and fleeting time, recruiters are becoming a necessity versus a luxury. By creating a vast network of hungry employers, all looking for qualified recruits, a savvy recruiter can always put the right employee together with the right employer.

And networking is what it's all about. "Well over 50 percent of jobs are found through networking and while working with a recruiter isn't technically networking, in a way it is," explains Christine Edick, a career coach at A Career Coach 4 U. "Recruiters have insight into jobs that are not even advertised, which gives them an advantage."

Think of the last time you performed a job search. The typical scenario is to place an ad, sift through a dozen, several dozen, and even dozens upon dozens of poorly-targeted, potentially under- or over-qualified resumes and hand-pick a short list that is then personally interviewed by you and your staff.

Not only is this time-consuming, it's time-wasting; recruiters sift through the resumes, applicants and even do the lion's share of interviewing for you, before it even gets to the meet and greet stage. This kind of filtering can only be found at the highest level of executive recruiting, and only by those qualified to know what you want, in many cases before you even do yourself.

Many of the best firms will provide background and reference checks for your candidates. Some will also, at an additional charge, complete personality and trait assessments. These are starting to become more of a norm for companies today as skill sets and competencies are clearly not enough. Employers want to know that a candidate will not only succeed in their new role, but also be a good match culturally.

Make the recruiter work hard to make certain that they are bringing the best and most qualified talent to you. But most of all maintain communication with your recruiter. Offer them feedback on candidates, so they know exactly your sticking points and how they can be more effective in the search.

By acting as a filter, the professional recruiter saves you time, money and turnover. Any one of these assets would be a significant savings in and of itself; all three combined are nothing short of priceless.

Quotes from the Corner Office:

By creating a vast network of hungry employers, all looking for qualified recruits, a savvy recruiter can always put the right employee together with the right employer.

TO MARKET, TO MARKET:
WHAT RECRUITERS KNOW THAT YOU DON'T

Assumptions can make or break a successful new hire. Assuming that the market is glutted when it's actually sparse, or even vice versa, can both affect hiring decisions. For instance, hiring out of need because of the perception that there are no good clients to be had in the local marketplace can often lead to rash decisions.

Likewise, being overly selective because of the expectation that there is always a better recruit out there in a market that doesn't really exist can mean passing up a good employee and being left with far fewer choices than one at first imagined. As I tell both candidates and clients, "Time kills all deals." If you are going to move, be resolute in your decision. That is why knowing what you want is important, but also knowing how to be realistic with the job market is even more so.

By knowing the market in real-time, versus fantasy time, professional recruiters take the guesswork out of the hiring process. Explains Kevin Wheeler, author of *The Corporate University Workbook*, "The competent recruiter is able to tell the hiring manager what the employment market looks like, what the supply of talent for a particular job is likely to be in her area, and how difficult it will be to find and close on candidates."

Many of my clients who have successful placements know that a recruiter must been seen not as an outside instigator but as an extension of the Human Resources Department. They are not simply a hired gun looking to make the quick placement. The good ones know that to be successful in today's marketplace means understanding the company and becoming a true working partner to find the best talent.

Unfortunately, too many companies view recruiters as used car salesmen looking to make a quick buck. Although that perception may still run true with lower-level firms, the really great firms know better than to treat a client poorly. As the client, you should expect a lot from your recruiter. Use them as a sounding board or get advice from them before you make a hiring decision. Because their outlook on your industry may make you think twice about any change.

Knowing *when* to hire is almost as important as knowing *who* to hire. The value of knowing the local market is in realizing when to walk, when to run and when to sprint! Busy leaders can often be out of touch with the hiring scene; busy recruiters never are!

Quotes from the Corner Office:

By knowing the market in real-time, versus fantasy time, professional recruiters take the guesswork out of the hiring process.

FREEING UP THE FLOW OF INFORMATION

Working with a recruiter is just that; work. No recruiter is an island unto himself, nor is any good leader. By working together, by collaborating in the efforts to produce quality hires that stay loyal, stay busy and, just as importantly, stay put, the quality recruiter is a commodity in and of himself.

But he must have the proper tools to do his job, and that's where you come in. Fitz O'Neill, an executive recruiter, and George Colberg, general manager of the Tampa office of MSI International, say, "Since recruiters are in the information business, the more information you can give them, the less time it will take to fill the position with the perfect candidate."

If you retain or hire a search firm, remember that even though that agency may be a "hired gun" for your company, they ultimately represent your company in the marketplace. Don't hold back resources or feedback for fear of giving away the store. Instead, give them the information about your company that you want them to use when they describe your company.

Honesty is the lifeblood of any smart hiring decision; honesty of purpose, honesty in advertising, honesty in expectations and honesty of information. The poorly-armed recruiter can unwittingly handpick the finest group of ill-fitting recruits ever assembled. The properly armed recruiter can make all the difference in providing the properly-qualified recruit.

Information alone is rarely enough. Recruiters operate in real-time and, as such, open lines of communication are vital to a successful placement. Make sure you have an open-door, open-phone and/or open-email policy with your recruiter so that you can provide constant feedback on candidates.

Letting the recruiter know about the company culture, the hiring authority's likes and dislikes, the overall financial outlook of the company, the confidentiality of the project, etc., are all important for a recruiter to portray your company in the best light.

The beauty of providing your recruiter with honest, timely and realistic information about your hiring needs is that the buck stops there; the onus of finding the right recruit to fit your demanding expectations rests solely on his or her shoulders.

Quotes from the Corner Office:

Honesty is the lifeblood of any smart hiring decision; honesty of purpose, honesty in advertising, honesty in expectations and honesty of information.

Pothole # 10:
Compromising on
Excellence

In the ongoing and endless quest for excellence, resourceful employers are pulling out all the stops to find excellent employees. Case in point: Bill Brooks, CEO at Brooks Group, a Greensboro, N.C., sales-management training firm, makes ample use of a personalized online assessment tool that touches on personal behaviors, attitudes, values and skills.

He uses this tool not just to assess compatibility between employee and employer, but to test for that ever-elusive hiring gem: excellence. "We have a whole series of assessments that we mix and match," says Brooks. "It's demanding and tough and fair." This quest does not come quickly or cheaply, but the rewards are Brooks Group's low employee turnover and high employee morale.

Assessment tools are just one of the many ways companies are targeting excellence in prospective new hires. In a competitive market, leaders must turn to competitive means of achieving excellence among new recruits.

Perhaps it's fitting that *Compromising on Excellence* is **Pothole # 10**. After all, don't all roads to success find excellence at their final destination? Unfortunately, many corporate hitchhikers are hired out of need versus specialty, and thus a quick-fix turns into a temporary one.

Excellence may be hard to come by, but it's well worth the wait. Unfortunately, few companies in today's competitive market can afford to wait quite that long—or quite that often. If this sounds like you—or even if it doesn't—this chapter will effectively arm you to seek out and hire excellence at any point along your company's hiring curve.

I know it's easy to settle for a "good enough" employee to fit the bill for a job right now. But good enough will only go so far, and soon enough they'll be looking for someplace else that's good enough—for them. My job is to keep those hitchhikers out of the corner office.

But I can only do it with your help.

Quotes from the Corner Office:

In a competitive market, leaders must turn to competitive means of achieving excellence among new recruits.

EXPECT EXCELLENCE; GET EXCELLENCE

Lou Holtz, one of America's winningest coaches, had much to say about excellence. One of his most relevant statements was, "I won't accept anything less than the best a player's capable of doing, and he has the right to expect the best that I can do for him and the team." Holtz didn't win games alone; he had a strong team behind him because he chose the strong team behind him.

Too often we let the team choose us. We hire out of a sense of need or even desperation. We hire based on looks, resume, a great interview or a great reference. We pinpoint glimmers of hope and ignore red flags that invariably pop up. We may avoid falling into the trap of hiring a bad employee, but how much better is hiring a merely mediocre or entirely adequate worker?

Excellence starts with us. It may be more challenging to search for excellence, it may take longer, it may cost more and produce less, but we didn't get to the executive level by taking the short trip to the quick-fix. Long-term gains require long-term commitments, and a commitment to excellence is the cornerstone of any successful hiring philosophy.

People have a way of rising to the occasion. When you demand excellence, you quite often get it. When you hire excellence, excellence results. Excellent new hires raise the bar for existing employees; they even raise the bar for future employees.

When word spreads that XYZ Company has the toughest interview methods, most demanding review process and a passion for excellence, the quality of your recruits will literally skyrocket.

Quotes from the Corner Office:

We may avoid falling into the trap of hiring a bad employee, but how much better is hiring a merely mediocre or entirely adequate worker?

EXCELLENCE AS A GOAL; EXCELLENCE AS THE RESULT

Excellence is more than just an idea or an expectation; excellence can be achieved. When you make excellence a goal and put steps into place to achieve that well-defined goal, excellence quickly evolves from some quasi-dreamlike state to an achievable reality.

But it doesn't happen by accident; it happens through careful planning and high expectations. As Howard Cowan notes in *Managers Magazine*, "To me, goal-setting and planning are the most important parts of the recruiting process. Without goals or a plan, you have no knowledge of where you are heading or how well you are doing."

Can excellence happen by accident? Sure; absolutely. Excellent recruits have been known to walk in off the street and get snatched up by some lucky company that improves simply from their presence, or so the urban legend goes.

But how profitable is fantasy versus reality?

Excellence will never be a priority for you if you continue to see it as a level of perfection not yet attained. Haven't you achieved excellence in your own career? Surely, that was no easy feat. Nor will it be for your new hires. Still, there is no better guide than a nurturing leader.

Make excellence a goal and show others how to achieve it. Too often we sacrifice excellence for mediocrity; the results are more hitchhikers, more empty offices, more hiring potholes and more costly recruiting practices.

Who ever thought it took *less* effort to strive for *more* excellence?

Quotes from the Corner Office:

When you make excellence a goal and put steps into place to achieve that goal, excellence evolves from some quasi-dreamlike state to an achievable reality.

ATTITUDE OVER APTITUDE

Hiring for excellence is not the same thing as hiring for perfection; one is readily-attainable, the other ever-elusive. As they say at Peter Barron Stark & Associates, "Hire for attitude, train for technical competence. If experience teaches you one thing as a manager, it is this: People with great attitudes are willing to learn whatever it takes to be successful in their positions. A technical expert with a bad attitude can ruin the motivation and attitude of the whole team."

Part of the *Compromising on Excellence* Pothole is the misdirected notion that a technically-skilled recruit is automatically an excellent asset. That may very well be true, but technical proficiency is only a piece of the professional puzzle. If the new hire's personal attitude doesn't equal, or even come close to, his or her technical proficiency, you'll never have more than a fraction of an employee.

Fractional employees make wholehearted hitchhikers; they always feel out of place and restless for the road that brings them somewhere where their technical skills are more valued than their personal skills. But technical skills are limited; they are only good as the software they manipulate, the hardware they master or the technology that evolves.

A positive and willing attitude is limitless; not only can it overcome any "technical difficulties" it may encounter, but it can inspire and motivate a cadre of colleagues who become eager to keep it around. Employees who are wanted want to stick around; the last thing they want to do is stick out their thumb and make a quick getaway.

Next time you are in a hiring position remember to factor attitude into your own personal excellence equation. It may not show up on a resume or even in an aptitude test, but if your quest is truly for excellence you'll know it when you see it.

Quotes from the Corner Office:

Hiring for excellence is not the same thing as hiring for perfection; one is readily-attainable, the other ever-elusive.

DON'T BE AFRAID OF DIVERSITY

Too often we equate excellence with our picture-perfect image of who meets our own criteria for distinction. Excellence is a feeling as much as anything else; we know it when we see it because when we see it we feel it. Too often, however, what we see in the mirror becomes our comfort zone.

Don't be afraid of diversity. The marketplace is full of talented individuals just itching for a chance to flourish; don't deny them the proper care and feeding they require simply because they don't look like the rest of your board.

In its "Tips for Making Great Hires" pamphlet series, Coca-Cola lists three vital criterion for hiring; something they call The Right "SET": Skills, Experience and Traits. As you ruminate on any new hire, make these the focus of your final decision, not your personal feelings about continuity and compatibility that may surface in your mind.

We all have comfort zones that operate on the subconscious level; diversity has a way of threatening our safety net, of tweaking our sense of what that corner office should look or feel like.

Diversity in the workplace is an asset, not a liability. Every new hire should be an opportunity for improvement, not simply a slot to fill to keep the status quo alive. What is the quest for excellence if not a quest for diversity? Like surprise packages, excellence comes in all kinds of shapes, colors, sizes and backgrounds.

When your corporate headquarters is full of people who look, think and act alike, performance can often be tracked on a safe and predictable path. When we step outside the box and hire with an eye for diversity, we recognize the value of others' thoughts and opinions and how they can bring a fresh, new perspective to nudge us off that safe plateau.

Diversity is not something to be feared but an opportunity to be embraced. Don't get me wrong; the best candidate for a job should always be hired regardless of—and not because of—his or her race, religion, culture or ethnicity. However, when we open up ourselves to the possibility that excellence comes in a wide variety of hues and backgrounds, we open ourselves—and our companies—up to a new and, quite possibly, excellent experience.

Quotes from the Corner Office:

*Excellence is a feeling as much as anything else; we know it when we see it because when we see it we **feel** it.*

Conclusion:
Boardroom or Bust!

Avoiding potholes isn't easy, but when you're in the driver's seat you're the only one who can make the difference between a bumpy ride and smooth sailing all the way to Destination Success. Hopefully, this guidebook has helped chart a course for a long, pothole-free ride straight to recruiting and retention success.

Along our journey we've hit some high points and low; we've witnessed the dangers of hiring poorly and felt the promise that comes with hiring properly. We all know that filling positions takes time, but when we make the time to install a step-by-step process that works not just for this new hire but for a lifetime of new hires, the payoff is higher retention and low turnover.

All books are created to fill one need or another; the need for adventure, self-help, romance, how-to or who-to or when-to or why-to. This book also arose from a need; the need for high-yield, low-effort, read-today, use-today steps to avoid a looming "hiring drought."

As a result, it's part how-to, who-to, when-to and a whole lot of why-to:

- **How-to ...** hire for maximum retention.

- **Who-to ...** hire for the right job at the right time.

- **When-to ...** hire out of want versus need.

- **Why-to ...** think about hiring before the need arises.

I hope this short, informative book has filled more than just a need to take this step or that, but has gone beyond to fill a greater need beyond today's—or even tomorrow's—next new hire.

What need?

That will be up to you, of course, but for my purposes if I have made you think about the hiring process for one month, one week or even one day more than you did last week, last month or last year, then I will have achieved my primary goal for putting pen to paper.

Thinking about hiring may not be enough, but it's a start.

Thought leads to action; action leads to results. The results I want for you are nothing short of floor after floor bursting with corner offices filled to overflowing for as long as the desk chairs hold up and the power stays on.

Every company should work to capacity, and yet too often we go far too long with far too few contributing to the greater cause. Empty offices mean overworked executives. Choosing the right new hire for you, for the company, for them has both an immediate and lasting impact. The less executives have to do the more they want to do; the more they want to do the better they do.

Help them do better by hiring better. The choice is yours: hire now or hire later. Slots have to be filled, desk chairs utilized and corner offices populated. Someone's going to occupy that office, sit in that chair and fill that slot. You're going to put them there. Hopefully, thanks to this book, you're going to KEEP them there.

After all, haven't we had just enough hitchhikers breeze through our corner offices to last a lifetime?

Quotes from the Corner Office:

Hopefully this guidebook has helped chart a course for a long, pothole-free ride straight to recruiting and retention success.

About the Author:
Orrick G. Nepomuceno, CPC

With over 20 years experience in the food and hospitality industry as a human resources consultant, pastry chef, and award-winning entrepreneur, Orrick has developed professional relations with many executives in the industry. He manages his own recruiting practice in conjunction with Dick Wray Executive Search, where he consults C-Level executives with Human Capital Resource issues. He understands the importance of helping companies build great teams to become successful in today's changing marketplace.

Orrick earned his Bachelor's Degree in Economics from Miami University in Oxford, Ohio and an Associate's Degree in Occupational Studies from the New England Culinary Institute in Essex, Vermont. He is also a Certified Personnel Consultant by the National Association of Personnel Services.

Orrick resides in Raleigh, North Carolina with his wife and two children.

978-0-595-43353-7
0-595-43353-7

www.ingramcontent.com/pod-product-compliance
Lightning Source LLC
Chambersburg PA
CBHW030839180526
45163CB00004B/1389